Memoirs of an
Everglades Pioneer

By Gertrude Petersen Winne

∽

Edited by Patricia Winne Adams

Editorial Rx Press
Orange Park, FL

A history of Florida publication published by Editorial Rx Press
Original cover and book layout design by Biographics

Editorial Rx Press, Registered Office:
P.O. Box 794,
Orange Park, FL, USA, 32067
www.editorialrxpress.com

First Editorial Rx Press Printing 2010

10 9 8 7 6 5 4 3 2 1

Library of Congress Cataloging in Publication Data

Winne, Gertrude Petersen, 1872-1972—author
Adams, Patricia Winne—editor
Memoirs of an Everglades Pioneer/Gertrude Petersen Winne;
Edited by Patricia Winne Adams.

p.   cm.

ISBN   978-0-9799274-7-8
1. Everglades Florida—History.
2. Florida—Pioneer experience.
3. Winne family.

Dedication

This book is dedicated with love and lots of thanks to Aunt Dorothea (Winne) Seiler and to Uncle Ross Winne, Jr., for their invaluable support in helping this project become a reality.

It is also dedicated in loving memory to Ross and Gertrude's other children, Wilton (Bill), 1911-1960; John (Jack), 1913-1938; Herman (Smiddy), 1916-1996; and Mary, 1921-1975.

My grandparents' story is of a life-long love affair. They loved each other, their family, and their Florida.

– Patricia Winne Adams

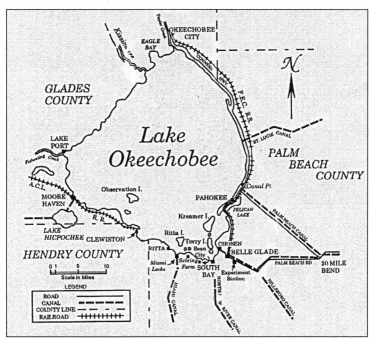

1928 map of Lake Okeechobee. Torry Island is on the southern end of the lake. Note: The Palm Beach County label is misplaced. North of Canal Point has been in Martin County since 1925.

Contents

Acknowledgment

I thank Editorial Rx Press for bringing my grandmother's words to life in this book—enabling others to experience the Florida that was and to see both courage and love in action. Deb Whippen, Publisher and Editor, provided wonderful guidance, Lori Alexander, President, shared her enthusiasm for this work from the beginning, Amy Boches, Biographics, applied her admirable graphic designer talents, Laura King copyedited the text with skill for maintaining with clarity my grandmother's voice, and Doug Byrnes ensured that the production quality of this book is top-notch on every page.

– Patricia Winne Adams, Editor

*"Pioneering the Everglades
was a man's paradise
and a woman's hell."*

— Gertrude Petersen Winne

Foreword

Florida in the early 1900s bore no resemblance at all to the heavily populated state seen in later years. Imagine a Florida with few navigable roads and limited rail travel. The Florida East Coast Railroad was still a vision in Henry Flagler's eye in the 1900s. The sturdy pioneers who came to Florida in this time experienced adventure and hardship. Some decided the harsh life of tropical southern Florida and the Lake Okeechobee area was too much for them to adapt to. These people did not linger long. Others, like Ross Winne, came to Florida to escape the cold winters of the north. Ross, in particular, came to continue his vocation as a commercial fisherman. He spent two winters in South Florida in the Miami area as a saltwater fisherman. He listened to stories of Lake Okeechobee and the wonderful freshwater fishing there. He quickly decided Lake Okeechobee was his land of the future. Ross returned to his home in Ohio and set about returning to Florida permanently.

Ross renewed old friendships and acquaintances during this time. Among the friends was Gertrude Petersen. She was the eighth of eleven children born to Julius Martin Petersen and Anna Dorothea (called Dora) Braun. Ross and Gertrude married on June 10, 1910, in Ottawa County, Ohio. Ross regaled "Gertie," as he called her, with stories of his visits to Florida and about his desire to return for the winter months. Gertrude agreed to go with Ross to Florida to camp and fish through the winter months. The preparations for the trip began in earnest as the young couple made lists of the supplies they could take with them that would provide the bare necessities. Their first-born child, Wilton, was born on April 23, 1911, in Bono, Ohio. Preparations for the trip to Florida were concluded, and the three of them, Ross, Gertie, and baby Wilton, set out for Florida in late 1911.

This book is based on the journals written by Gertie, who was my paternal grandmother. I grew up hearing stories told by my grandmother and my father Herman, along with my aunts and uncles, about the early years on Lake Okeechobee. My aunt, Mary Winne Josephson, transcribed the journals into typewritten draft prior to her death in 1975. The typewritten draft was given to me by my father in 1992. It was always my desire to share my grandmother's vivid story with readers interested in the historical stories of early Florida.

The original journals were returned to Dorothea Winne Seiler after Mary's death and in turn, Aunt Dorothea gave me these writings in late 2009. Reviewing her words and reliving the gamut of emotions she experienced as a young woman in a wild and untamed Florida wilderness and the later horror, tragedy, and hardship she and Ross experienced in the devastating 1928 hurricane and again in the 1949 storm brought tears to my eyes more than once. I am still amazed at the courage and the strength of the woman I knew and loved.

It took the most courageous of women to brave the unknown wilds of the Florida wilderness. This is her story. Let her tell it to you.

– Patricia Winne Adams, Editor
Granddaughter of Gertrude P. Winne

Part I

Torry Island, Florida
1910-1913

The BLUE HORSE
No. 518
COMPOSITION BOOK
QUALITY—QUANTITY

Book list

Begining the What-is-it —

Many, many times these last few years
I have quietly sat thinking back over
the years since I first came to Fla.
and wondered about the complaining
people of today, these people who have
air planes, motor cars, telephones, and
all the modern conveniences and
the pleasure of near by neighbors and
friends, always some one near to
lend a helping hand and the Drs.
and modern hospitals in case of
sickness or accident, then I go
back to the first years that I spent
on an island in Lake Okeechobee
when there were no conveniences or
neighbors + transportation was
almost no transportation at all.
I wonder what these complaining
people would have done had they
lived here then.

1

Into the Unknown

Many times during the last few years I have quietly sat thinking about the years since I first came to Florida and wondering about the complaining people of today, people who have airplanes, motor cars, telephones, modern conveniences, the pleasure of nearby neighbors and friends, and doctors and modern hospitals in case of sickness or accidents. Then I recall the first years that I spent on an island on Lake Okeechobee during a time when there were no conveniences, no neighbors, and only boat transportation. I wonder what these complaining people would have done had they lived here then.

I have often been urged to write about those early days but never felt that I could assemble my memories sufficiently to put them down on paper until now. This is not fiction but reality. I shall relate to you the events of my life in the sequence and manner in which they occurred, with whatever horror or beauty the passing days showered upon us.

Goodbye, Ohio

I have always considered myself fortunate for having been reared on a farm in the beautiful Black Swamp country of northern Ohio. Much of the land there had to be drained and was a rich, black muck. Lake Erie with its lovely, shady beach was less than a mile from my home, and folks from far and near would come to spend their summer Sundays and holidays there, which made the place quite a popular summer resort and afforded the local young folks with plenty of recreation. The long winter evenings were spent gathered in various homes for popping corn, pulling candy, and dancing. To us, loneliness was just a word in the dictionary.

At the age of 18, I was married to a young man named Ross from one of the local families. Ross had spent most of his adult life on the Great Lakes and, at the time of our marriage in 1910, was a fisherman. He so disliked the long, cold winters of the north that during the winter before our marriage he decided to try the salt water fishing in Miami, Florida. After spending that first winter in Florida, he said there would be no more cold winters for him. While in Miami, he heard the fishermen talk of fishing on Lake Okeechobee, which was a fresh water lake. Because he didn't care for salt water fishing, he asked a great many questions about the fishing on Lake Okeechobee but was unable to get any concrete information about it because the lake was remote from Miami in those days. To get from Miami to the lake, you had to go by train up the east coast to Palatka, then across the state to Fort Myers. At Fort Myers, you had to take the boat down to the lake, that is, if there was a boat available. Being a stranger and not knowing the state very well, Ross was confused by this, so when the next wintertime came, the first winter after our marriage, he again went to Miami, not only to get away from the cold but also to learn as much as possible about Lake Okeechobee and the fresh water fishing. He returned to Ohio the first of March fully determined to go to Lake Okeechobee for the fresh water fishing the next winter.

Our baby son was born on Sunday, April 23, 1911, and we named him Wilton. The summer was hot and dreadfully windy, so when winter began showering her icy blasts upon us, the man of the house began making preparations for the trip to Florida, this time bringing the baby and me with him. Despite all the hustle and bustle, it was late in December before we were finally ready to start, and it was with mixed feelings that I packed our trunks for our trip into the unknown. Unknown it really was, and if I could have had one tiny peek into the immediate future, I doubt very much if I would ever have left my beloved Ohio.

Florida: Here We Come

No mere pen could even begin to tell of the frightening things, the heartaches, and the utter, utter loneliness for a woman going through those endless days and weeks and years. I had heard so much of the beauties of Florida—the wonderful climate, with its summer the year round, the stately palm trees, the beautiful flowers, and many other wonders—that it seemed like gilding a lily, and although I was skeptical about it all, still I was willing to be shown; so putting my best foot forward and with all of the determination I could command, we sallied forth to anything but the paradise I was supposedly to find.

The trip from Toledo to Jacksonville was monotonous and uneventful. We had a few hours between trains in Jacksonville, so we set out to see a bit of the town, which turned out to be disappointing. After all these years, what I remember most clearly was the place where fish sandwiches were sold to the black people. These places were no more than a roof over a box wedged in a narrow space between buildings or perhaps under a stairway. The front of the place was made in such a way that the upper part was hinged to the lower about breast high; this hinged part opened outward and was propped up to form a shelf. On this shelf would be a large pile of fried fish, the fish having been cooked on an oil stove at the back of the box. When a customer stopped by for a sandwich, a fish was taken from the pile, placed between two slices of bread with some sort of sauce spread on them, and that was the sandwich.

I couldn't help thinking how unsanitary it all was: no screens, flies all over, and the dust from the street settled on everything. The place had such a rancid, greasy, fishy smell, with, now and then, a spoiled fish thrown in for good measure. The garbage from the place was in an open can beside the sidewalk at the end of the shelf laden with the fried fish. If we sauntered through any of Jacksonville's many beauty spots that day they were wasted on me because I saw this other place first.

Train time finally came, and we got on board and settled ourselves for the ride down to Palatka. The coaches on the Florida trains at that time were the outmoded coaches discarded by the other railroads. The coaches on this train were narrow, and the seats were covered with a straw-like matting that was so slippery you had to be continually pushing yourself back onto the seat to keep from sliding onto the floor. The weather was dreadfully hot, and looking out of the windows, we could see the white sand, which reminded us of the snow we had left back home and only helped to make the day seem hotter. Naturally, in all that heat we soon became thirsty, so we headed off to the water cooler at the end of the coach; it was as dry as we were. While we were debating the possibilities of water being available in any of the other coaches, the conductor came through, so we asked him about it. He told us there was no water on the train. The train workers at Jacksonville had forgotten to put water in the coolers, as well as the ice. No water and hours to Palatka. Our throats were parched.

This was the day before Christmas, and in my discomfort I couldn't help thinking about home and imagining what was going on there. The tree would have been trimmed the night before, but Mother would be getting the bird ready for roasting tomorrow. The girls would be baking cakes and cookies, making candy and popcorn balls. Dad would be getting the nuts from the attic, apples and pears from the cellar, and many other things he was wont to do the day before Christmas. But here we were in a strange country, the baby fretful, and all of us uncomfortable. Oh, for a drink of good, cool water. It would have meant so much right then, and it was all I could do to keep back the tears.

Nearly sundown. Palatka at last and that long desired drink of water. How wonderful and satisfying a drink of water can be.

When we left Toledo, we brought a basket of lunch with us, including a quart jar of canned fruit. The jar was empty now, so I carefully rinsed it out and filled it with water on the next leg of our trip, just in case the train was again dry. How welcome that quart of water was because once again the water coolers on the train were empty.

Our stop in Palatka was but a few minutes; just as the sun was going down we pulled out and headed west across the state toward Lakeland, which was to be our next stop. It was Christmas Eve, and the train was crowded. We finally got our baggage piled between our seats to be used for footrests and again tried to make ourselves comfortable in the most uncomfortable seats that ever were built.

Exiting Palatka, we were soon in the pine forests. Looking out of the train window, trying to catch a glimpse of the sunset through those towering pine trees, I caught my breath and thought, "How beautiful." The rich green of the pine against the vivid colors of that sunset was beyond description. It was the first beautiful thing I had seen in Florida, and I thought of how discomforts are manmade, but only God could make such natural beauty. So I settled down with a tiny speck of contentment. My contentment, however, was short-lived. Timber like that calls for sawmills; sawmills mean men, mostly rough men, and such was the group who came aboard the train at Palatka. They had evidently gone to town for some holiday cheer and had imbibed well but unwisely. In the crowd and heat of the train, what started out to be cheer turned to quarrelsomeness, and soon those men were fighting, and the entire train was in an uproar. There was no place to go to get away from the ugly words and angry, fighting men. The only thing to do was to try to sit quietly and pretend not to notice.

The conductor came through and tried to stop them, but it was beyond him, so he went off to gather his fellow workers to lend assistance. While he was gone, one of the men was badly stabbed and thrown from the train. The conductors soon returned, armed with guns and billy clubs. They subdued the gang and wired ahead for officers to meet the train at the next stop, where the rowdies were taken from the train. I have always wondered what happened to the man who was stabbed and thrown from that moving train, out into the middle of nowhere.

Also in our coach was a tiny, elderly lady, perhaps 75 years old, accompanied by a grandson of about 14. We all noticed how the boy tried to shield his grandmother to keep her from seeing the rough-and-tumble fighting that was going on in the end of the coach. He talked to her almost constantly as if to try to keep her from hearing the ugly language being used. Despite the boy's efforts, we all could see that the little lady was very excited and nervous. Not long after the fighting men had been removed from the train, she slumped down in the seat half conscious and looked so very strange.

The grandson was frightened. He dug frantically into his grand-mother's handbag and brought out a small bottle of tablets to try to give her one, but there was no water on the train except the precious little I still had in my quart jar. I brought my jar to him and helped him give the tablet to his grandmother. Then we moistened handkerchiefs and placed them on her forehead and wrists, piled luggage between the two seats, and laid her down as best we could. After a while she responded to the medicine and by morning seemed quite recovered.

Morning! How wonderful it was to see daylight come peeping through those smoke-begrimed windows, trying to blot out the memory of that awful night. What a Christmas morning that was. That morning and through that whole long day I never once heard the words "Merry Christmas." No happy faces to be seen anywhere. People all seemed grimly determined to get somewhere somehow and gave no signs that they might even be remembering that this was the day of days, the birthday of Christ.

The sun rose bright and clear, and the country we were now passing through was dotted with clumps of pine trees, an occasional palm hammock, and myrtle scrub, with lakes everywhere. Once we saw a wild deer racing madly for cover. What a contrast this part of the state was to that we had passed through the afternoon before, and this was my first glimpse of the cabbage palmetto.

We breakfasted in Lakeland, but our time there was so short we saw nothing of the town and were soon on another train heading for Fort Myers, the end of the line—not only the end of that line, but

Fort Myers was the southernmost town on the West Coast to have railroad accommodations at that time. We arrived there at noon, tired, hot, dirty, and thirsty. The water coolers on the train were as dry as all the others had been, and we had neglected to fill our jar with water at Lakeland.

On the station platform, we started discussing the possibilities of hotel accommodations, when a tall, gray-haired man stepped up and, doffing a 10-gallon sombrero, made a courtly bow, introduced himself, and drawled, "If you all are looking for a boarding hotel, I own a small place about a block and a half from here." He quoted prices and said if we were interested he would be proud to see that our luggage got down there right away. Of course we were interested. That bit of courtesy after the trip down from Jacksonville seemed like a bit of heaven, and it was good to know that we were going to stay put for a few days anyway.

The little place turned out to be little indeed: an old residence with a room or two added here or there, with more thought given to the need for more room than to adding anything to the external appearance of the house. The house, although none too pleasing to the eye, was built in the center of a large lot and was surrounded by seedling orange and grapefruit trees, the tallest I have ever seen anywhere, which bore delicious fruit.

The baths we had looked forward to were disappointing. There was no bathroom. In the rooms were old-fashioned washbowls with a pitcher of water. In the backyard, there were two privies, one marked *Ladies*, the other *Men*. Everything was very neat and clean, which was gratifying; so making the best of what we had, we freshened ourselves as quickly as possible and hurried out to our Christmas dinner. What a strange dinner it seemed to us—the main dish being the traditional collard greens with hog jowls (I had never heard of it before) and plain boiled rice. One would have had no difficulty in sorting out who was who around the tables. All the Southerners fell to and were stowing this food away with great dispatch, while we "Damn Yankees" weren't having anything, except the cornbread, which was delicious. The other northerners, like myself, had settled down to make a meal of cornbread, but soon we were delightfully surprised when a regular Christmas dinner followed, which we thoroughly enjoyed.

After dinner the baby was ready for his nap and was soon asleep. Being very tired ourselves, Ross and I decided we could do with a bit of rest too, so we were soon as fast asleep as the baby, but not for long. We were awakened by a great deal of loud popping, as though many pistols were being shot off at once. Rushing out to learn what the shooting was about, we felt foolish when we were told it was only firecrackers. "Firecrackers?" I said, "On Christmas?" "Oh, yes, indeed, ma'am," said our host. "And tonight there will be a fireworks display put on by the town that you will be able to see from the front verandah." We were dumbfounded. Firecrackers to us meant the Fourth of July. However, it turned out to be a very beautiful display of fireworks. And so ended the strangest Christmas day of my whole life.

The next day Ross, in the company of Henry Bodi, a man from Toledo who was to be his fishing partner, set out to see what they could learn about the fish business in the town and about boats and boat transportation to Lake Okeechobee. They returned late in the morning and told me that they were going to have to build a boat because there was none to be bought. In addition, the fishing gear and equipment that they had shipped from Toledo hadn't arrived, so it would be a week or 10 days before we could go on the lake.

Our host at the hotel, on hearing that Ross and Mr. Bodi were going to build a boat, told them that they could build it there in the yard under the orange trees if they cared to. This was welcomed by the men, a place to work in the shade instead of in the hot sun down on the waterfront, so as soon as dinner was over, they hurried out to buy the materials. The materials were delivered before night and early the next morning found the two men working away at their boat building job.

Mr. Bodi and his wife Mary decided to move to our little hotel, as much in appreciation of the kindness of our host as to be handy to work. I had thought how nice it would be to have them there; it would give us a chance to get acquainted before setting out on our camping trip to the lake, and it would be nice to have someone to go see the town with. I had met Mary Bodi only a few times before, although Ross had known both of them for many years. I was sadly disappointed, however, because Mary certainly was not the type of person who I would enjoy chumming around with, and even worse she did not like babies. She had a disagreeable disposition and a sharp tongue. She made no effort to be courteous and was altogether of a sour disposition. What an ordeal a camping trip with a person like that was going to be.

Living next door to the hotel were an old couple, Mr. and Mrs. Sellers; he was from Texas, and she was a Florida cracker. Both fell in love with my little son Wilton, and they were both very kind to us. They asked me to stay at their house as much as possible so they could have the baby there. Wilton enjoyed their house because he could get down on the floor to creep around and play. I was delighted over their kindness because the baby had been crawling and pulling up on things long before we left Ohio, so he wasn't enjoying being held or kept on the bed all day. It was impossible to put him down in the hotel with all of those dirty, sandy feet tracking in and out all day. So, availing myself of their kind offer, I spent many hours of relaxation with the Sellers, time that otherwise would have been an ordeal.

When Ross had a few leisure moments, he too was wont to stroll over and sit on the porch for a quiet chat. The Sellers told us a great many things about Florida, particularly, Fort Myers. We learned from them that the only water works in the town was owned and operated by the big hotel, the Royal Palm, and the plant, being a small one, could accommodate only the main places of business besides the hotel; hence, no city water for any of the smaller hotels. We also learned that Thomas Edison, Henry Ford, and Harvey Firestone were just starting their plans for rubber experiments somewhere near Fort Myers and that Edison already had his home there.

Fort Myers was also a cow town. One day there was quite a lot of excitement in the town. A cattle boat from Key West had arrived. Live cattle were put on board these boats, along with enough feed not only for the trip but also to keep the cows well fed until they were butchered. In Key West, the cattle were kept in pens and butchered as needed. This was the only means of having fresh meat. Mechanical refrigeration was practically unknown in 1912. The East Coast Railroad had not yet been completed to Key West, and the hurricane of September 1910 had washed away several bridges, as well as the large houseboat on which the laborers were housed. Many lives were lost; I don't think it was ever definitely determined how many.

In due time the men finished their boat and put it into the water; the fishing gear arrived from Toledo and the steam boat from Lake Okeechobee. We learned that the boat would leave on New Year's Day at noon for the return trip to the lake, and we were to be ready to go with it.

When the old couple next door heard that we were leaving so soon, they tried to discourage me from going and taking the baby. It was 135 miles to Torry Island on a boat that ordinarily traveled about six miles an hour, but on this trip there were to be two loaded skiff boats in tow, which would cut the speed to less than five miles an hour.

We were told of the panthers, wild cats, wild hogs, and snakes! There were a lot of rattlesnakes on the sand land but none on the lake. It seems that rattlesnakes don't like the muck or swampy country, but the moccasins were plentiful and gave no warning; they would just lay invisible against the black muck and strike anything or anybody who came by. Worst of all was the kind of people who were down on the lake, mostly outlaws who had escaped the chain gang or others who had committed crimes and were hiding from the law. Not far away, at Taylor Creek, a murder had been committed. A man named Johnson had killed a man named White over a card game, and Johnson was in jail at Fort Myers, awaiting trial.

This and much more we heard; then, finally, "Those awful chiggers!" Tiny red bugs that burrow into the skin and raise a red bump that itches like fury. These were so thick on the foliage and in the muck that one couldn't possibly escape them. They would get on us all, especially the baby, and we would be miserable.

All this was, to say the least, not encouraging; in fact, it was terrifying. If there had been any part of me lower than the bottoms of my feet, that's where my heart would have been. Our finances were practically depleted, so there was nothing for me to do but to go along to Lake Okeechobee with the others and try to make the best of it, hoping that things wouldn't be as dreadful as the Sellers said they would be.

Mr. and Mrs. Sellers invited us to have Sunday dinner with them (Sunday being our last day at Fort Myers). A friend of theirs had just returned from a hunting trip and had given them some venison. Because we had never eaten venison, the Sellers were anxious to know how we would like it. It was delicious, and we expressed a hope that there might be deer down on the lake; however, we were disappointed in this because it seemed that the deer didn't care for the swampy country.

During the week that we had been making the Sellers' home our haven, we hadn't learned that Mr. Sellers was a convict guard. He had charge of a group of state convicts who were housed in a converted boxcar on the outskirts of town not very far from the Sellers' home. We had heard that the men who guarded convicts were cruel to the men, but we were in for a big surprise. I had never seen a convict before. In Ohio, the convicts either worked inside buildings or were screened from the public by a high board fence, but here in Florida, they worked out in public view. The particular men Mr. Sellers was in charge of were working on a state highway. After dinner, as we were all seated in the yard, one of these convicts came walking down the street. Mr. Sellers called him by name and said, "Haven't you any other clean clothes besides those?" "Yes, sir," said the convict. "Then go and put them on. Don't you know this is Sunday?" Whereupon the convict raced back to quarters and soon returned with civilian clothing on. "That's better," said Mr. Sellers. "Now you can go on uptown." Said I, "But I thought you kept them locked up when they aren't working." "No," he said. "I only lock them up at night to comply with the law. They are always on hand to work come Monday morning."

What a wonderful day this had been. Because of an old couple's love for our baby and their true Southern hospitality, we had been given the privilege of not only spending time in their home for the past week but also sharing this last day of 1911 with them. As we enjoyed the bounteous noontime meal and the long lazy afternoon with its friendly chatter, we felt like one of the family. Perfect, except for the nagging fear of what lay ahead on the morrow when we were again to venture out into God only knew what.

New Year, New Horizons

Now tomorrow was today, the first of the new year. Instead of the usual festivities, we were busily packing and making ready to leave immediately after dinner on our trip down to the lake. I was anything but happy and had to force myself to eat my New Year's dinner for I knew not when or where my next meal would be eaten. Our belongings had been taken to the boat before noon, so as soon as we had finished our dinner, we headed out to the dock to board the boat that would take us to Torry Island.

I hadn't as yet seen the boat, Mabel by name. When we stopped beside a boat and Ross said, "This is it," I couldn't believe my eyes. My first thought was, "How will we ever make such a long trip on that!" I had never seen anything like it. A flat bottom boat perhaps 36 feet long. Built in the bow was a large gas tank to supply fuel for the motor; behind the fuel tank was the ice-box, possibly 12 or 14 feet long, built right into the boat. Behind this, the cabin, about 8 feet long. This cabin housed the motor and tiller wheel. Across the front of the cabin were glass windows to provide visibility for steering the boat. Along either side were hinged bunks turned up when the boat was running and let down for sleeping when the boat was at anchor. The deck at the rear of the cabin was about 6 or 8 feet, and on this deck were several drums of gasoline being taken to the lake for various fishermen that the boat supplied with fuel and food. On the return trip, the boat would haul their fish back to market.

The ice-box was filled with ice—as all ice-boxes should be—to keep the fish from spoiling en route to the market. Atop the ice-box was piled as much of our belongings as possible, while towing astern were the two skiff boats, loaded down with fishing gear and camping things. There was no comfortable place to sit anywhere, and me with a baby to hold. At last I managed to find a cramped space on top of the ice-box where I sat cross-legged and held the baby.

Not knowing what I would be up against, I hadn't provided myself with a sun hat, so just as we were leaving, Mrs. Sellers, bless her heart, rushed out with her old yard hat, a cheap straw hat such as children wear on farms in summer, and urged me to take it, saying she could get another for herself tomorrow. What a blessing that bit of a straw hat was! The sun was bright and hot and no shade for the baby and me except that hat, so I did my best, twisting and turning while the boat wound its way down the crooked river, the Caloosahatchee, just about the most crooked river in the world.

At Fort Myers, the river is very wide and the water is brackish tidewater from the Gulf of Mexico. Later on, the water is fresh, and as the boat operated in fresh water except for this short distance, it did not carry drinking water on board but depended on keeping up a supply with a bucket tied to a rope. As long as we were running through brackish water, we weren't supposed to get thirsty, and if we did, we just had to wait until the boat came into the fresh water that was fit for drinking. The day being hot and the boat very slow, we all got thirsty long before the boat and the fresh water met.

Along with Mr. and Mrs. Bodi, Ross and son, and myself, there were 9 other people on board the boat, including the captain and his mate. Although the trip was long and we were in tight quarters, we barely spoke to one another during our voyage. Perhaps all our efforts went into just surviving the trip. It is bad enough to have to sit on a hard, flat surface at any time but to try to hold a squirming baby is something else again. Soon my legs were numb, and there was a violent pain in my back. I had little energy left to chat with my travel companions.

After an hour, the river narrowed and began looking more like a river than a bay. The banks on either side were covered with tall palm trees, with an occasional grove of live oaks, their limbs stretching out over the water gracefully hung with Spanish moss. Nestled in the moss were air plants and tree orchids in bloom, colorful and very beautiful, lovely enough to make me forget my discomforts for a while.

The chugging away of the motor and slow progress of the boat became monotonous indeed as the afternoon wore on. When the sun began to get low in the west, I began to wonder how we would ever manage anything to eat before darkness, but manage a bite we did. A small can of pork and beans was opened for each of us and a few boxes of crackers passed around. We ate the beans cold from the can, using a little wooden spoon, and that was supper. Not especially filling and definitely not satisfying.

There was no toilet on the boat, and after an entire afternoon of riding, we were all feeling the need of a relief station somewhere soon; but there we sat and squirmed in discomfort until about 10 o'clock that night when the motor was stopped and the boat nosed up to the bank. The captain said we would camp there the rest of the night. I heaved a great sigh of relief, happy at the thought of getting off that awful, uncomfortable boat for a few hours; but when I tried to stand up, my legs were so numb they refused to hold me. If Ross hadn't been beside me, I would have pitched overboard headfirst, and I could not swim a stroke.

I finally managed to get a little circulation in my legs and got ashore. It seemed so good to feel the good earth underfoot and to be able to walk up and down the bank a bit to get the kinks out of my legs and back. On looking about me, I saw that we were in a small clearing in a grove of palm trees. The men soon had a campfire going and coffee on to cook. A tent was stretched between two palm trees with a part of it spread on the ground for a floor. In this shelter, we put down a mattress on which we were to sleep the rest of the night.

It was so good to lie down and stretch after that back-breaking ride. Ross and the baby were soon asleep, but sleep would not come to me. I heard all of the noises of the woods nightlife and imagined I could hear rattlesnakes slithering about and was frightened for fear they would try to make bedfellows of us. In Fort Myers, we had been told of various hunters who had wakened to find rattlesnakes in their beds, so instead of sleeping as I should, I spent the night watching over my baby to make sure no snake made a bedfellow of him.

We were all astir long before sunup and managed to have a cup of coffee and a bit of cold canned food for breakfast before boarding the boat. During the night, net stakes had been loaded on the boat, so now there really was no place to sit except on those metal fuel drums on the stern of the boat. Those, with the rims extending an inch or more beyond the end of the drum, were the most uncomfortable yet. Mrs. Bodi and I would sit on them until we were sure our legs were almost cut off, then would slide off them to stand uncomfortably in a tiny space between the drums. From early morning all through the day it was the same—sit, stand, and sit again, until I felt I would go mad.

We passed through LaBelle very early in the morning and that was practically the last of civilization. Then for many miles there were cattle grazing on either side of the river and, occasionally, a few wild deer feeding with the cattle. About noon we stopped at a place where a small palmetto thicket grew down to the river's edge. My baby was asleep, and the captain very kindly lowered one of the bunks so I could lay him down for the little while we were stopping there.

It seemed a long time since morning, and nature was making demands on all of us. We scattered out in that small thicket, each one looking for a clump of bushes large enough to afford privacy. I found a heavy clump of palmetto and looked all about to make sure I was unobserved when I heard a crackling of brush, and craning my neck to peer around the bushes, I looked into Ross's face not 3 feet from me. What a good laugh we had at each other and ourselves.

Lunch was very light that day, consisting mostly of coffee. When the net stakes were loaded in the early morning, no one thought to get out anything for the day's rations. The groceries being stowed in the hold by the gas tank and the net stakes piled on the entire front of the boat, it was impossible to get any groceries out until the net stakes were unloaded. We were out in the middle of nowhere with hours yet to go and all of the food carefully stowed away and impossible to retrieve.

And so on we chugged toward Lake Okeechobee. As the afternoon wore on, the Caloosahatchee River became a canal and sundown found us tied up at a bit of canal bank on the western shore of Lake Hicpochee cooking our supper, which consisted of coffee, period. We were all hungry, and the baby, accustomed to three meals a day, was hungry, tired, and cross, which didn't make it any easier for me.

The country was all swamp and under water. The only way we could tell that we were entering Lake Hicpochee was by the ending of the canal banks. This lake is small and is connected with Lake Okeechobee by a 3-mile canal.

About nine o'clock we stopped at a camp on the 3-mile canal where Moore Haven now stands. The country here was under water too. The camp was built on pilings, and boats were tied up to the doorsteps. Some of the gasoline and a few provisions were unloaded here. Then we were again on our way, this time headed out across Lake Okeechobee. I was too utterly weary to know if I was sorry or glad.

The night was very dark. When we were well out in open water, a brisk northeast wind chopped up the waves and everyone was worried. The boat was considerably overloaded, and the skiff boats in tow were also heavily loaded. One man was kept busy pumping water from the skiffs to keep them from being swamped.

All things come to an end sometime, and this awful trip finally ended at 3 o'clock in the morning of January 3, 1912. Torry Island at last, and it was high and dry. What a relief that was. After so much swampy country, I was beginning to wonder if I was going to have to live over the water like those other folks, with a boat tied to my doorstep. Doorstep, did I say? It was many days before I had even a semblance of one.

2

Snakes and Other Wild Things

Torry Island

We approached the island from the west. About midway of the western shore, we entered a good-sized creek, which we traveled up for about a quarter-mile. Then we stopped, tied the boat to the bank, and all scrambled ashore. Here was a permanent fish camp owned by a Mr. Simmons and his son, Ed. Ed had been one of the passengers on the boat with us, and I hadn't even met or spoken to him. Now as I write this, it seems fantastic to think of being on that small boat for all those tiresome hours and interacting with only the captain and his mate. Except for Mr. and Mrs. Bodi, the rest of the people were still strangers to me. In those days, a lady never spoke to strangers, and Southern men never spoke to a lady unless properly introduced.

By the time we were all ashore, Mr. Simmons came out of his cabin, or shack as it was called, carrying a lighted lantern. He asked us to come in. Some of the people had their own tents pitched nearby, so they went on to their own places, but the rest of us, including the captain and his helper, accepted Mr. Simmons' invitation and went inside.

The shack was about 14 by 18 feet and consisted of a framework covered with tar paper. Everything was very neat and clean. At one end were two beds, and at the other, the stove and table. The legs of the table stood in cans of water to keep ants out of the food.

My baby had awakened and was fretting, so Mr. Simmons kindly asked me to lay him on the bed and sit by him. How good to be able to stretch my arms and rest my aching back. The baby rolled and kicked and laughed, so I knew that getting out of my arms was a relief to him too.

At the other end of the shack, Ed and his father were busily preparing a meal. The smell of that cooking food made me realize how hungry I was. We hadn't eaten a real meal since New Year's Day at noon, and I couldn't imagine how we could ever hope to get to our cooking things before morning. After moving around a bit and having a stretch, the men had gone out to unload the boats, trying to get things in shape to set a few nets when daylight came. After an hour or so, the boats were unloaded and the men from the boat came in, asking permission to wash up. Mr. Simmons showed them where to find the wash basin, soap, and water and gave them a clean towel, admonishing them to "Hurry up, please, supper is ready." They had cooked enough for all of us, a group of total strangers.

We were all dreadfully hungry. Even the baby had to be fed. As we sat around that table, I silently gave thanks for the kindness and generosity of these good people who were to be my neighbors and friends. When supper was finished, I offered to wash the dishes and clean up, but Mr. Simmons said, "No, let them go till morning. You all are tired now and should be in bed."

In bed, indeed, thought I. What bed and where? That problem, too, was solved for us. A man from Michigan, Joe Perry, had put up a tent that day but hadn't moved into it yet, so he offered us the use of his tent until we could get ours up. He stayed with the Simmons. The men got our mattresses and put them in the tent and I took a couple of blankets from our trunk. We were soon asleep, too tired to think about snakes and other wild things.

After a few hours of rest it was time to get up again. It seemed as though we had just lain down. Mr. Simmons and Ed had breakfast waiting for us. All the way from Fort Myers I had lived in fear and dread of the people I would meet on Lake Okeechobee. Instead of the escaped convicts and outlaws I was expecting, we found people like this.

It wasn't yet daylight when we trekked back over to breakfast, and I was soon anxious for daylight to come so I could see just what sort of place this Torry Island was. After breakfast, Mr. Simmons looked after the baby, and I washed the dishes and swept the floor, and during these household chores, we got a little acquainted.

Mr. Simmons was called "Dad" by most folks who knew him. Soon we were calling him Dad too. Dad's Southern drawl, his slurring of the letter R, and his quaint way of expressing himself fascinated me. I was soon asking questions and talking away at a great rate, which was unusual for me, because I had always been quite shy.

One of the first things he said to me that morning was, "You know, ma'am, I just love a little old baby, and this is the first one I have seen in more than a year." How odd to speak of a baby as "little old." He told me he hadn't been away from the island for more than 6 months. I asked him if he didn't get lonely, and he said, "No ma'am, a man as old as I am don't git lonesome; he has too many good memories to keep him company."

By now it was daylight outside ("good day" the Crackers call it), so, taking the baby in my arms, I went outside for a look around and encountered a surprise. Around the shack was a clearing of perhaps two acres; within this area, besides the shack, were three tents, one a huge affair in which Mr. and Mrs. Doss and their two children lived. Mr. Fix lived in the second, and the third was the one we had occupied. Dad Simmons told us that we could put our tents in his clearing too if we liked, and we gratefully accepted the offer.

The trees were unlike any I had ever seen before. They were short and spreading, with roots above the ground for 3 to 5 feet around the tree. The wood was spongy and cork-like, good for whittling but not for a campfire. We used it, however, because there was none other to be had. The trees grew right down to the water's edge and were mostly covered with a heavy vine bearing huge white flowers that smelled very sweet in the morning air. When the sun came up, the blossoms closed. Dad Simmons told me that the trees were custard apples and the flowering vines were moon vines. The blossoms would open again when the sun went down.

While I was busy with the breakfast dishes and with sweeping, Mrs. Bodi had been trying to untangle our camping equipment. The men had long since gone out to set the nets. I was anxious to get at our camping things too, but what to do with the baby? The soil was black muck with not a patch of grass on it, so I couldn't think of fixing a place for him on the ground. Moreover, there were chiggers (or red bugs) to consider. Dad said that they were plentiful. At last I hit on the idea of tucking him into one of the metal wash tubs; so folding a blanket, I arranged what was to be his play pen for many a day.

With the baby safely settled, Mrs. Bodi and I set to work fixing a place where we could cook our meals so we wouldn't have to impose on Dad and Ed any more. We had two tents, one for cooking and eating and the other for sleeping. The latter was to have a floor if ever the men took time off to build it.

Between the two of us, we managed to tie part of one of the tents between two trees so as to protect our oil stove from the wind and to afford shade from the hot sun while cooking. We pushed two trunks together and used the flat tops for a table. We had bought our canned goods by the case, so we used the wooden boxes for seats. We felt that we were quite well set up and hoped the weather would stay clear until the men got their nets set and our tents decently pitched. We were very fortunate to have had good weather, not for just a few days, but for several weeks. Even so, it was a week before we finally got the tents up, and it was so good at last to have a floor under our beds.

When our husbands came in from setting out their first string of nets, they were surprised to see how we had set up our housekeeping. We had a full meal cooked for them, even hot biscuits. They made a dreadful mistake that evening, though. They were so late getting in for supper that we had to eat by lantern light. The pesky bugs were into everything. We didn't waste any time getting our weary selves to bed that night and I resolved not to stay awake looking for trouble. If snakes and other critters crawled into bed with us, we would just take care of those things when they happened.

Sometime in the night we were all awakened by the weirdest noise I had ever heard. Frightened out of my senses, I sat up in bed, snatched up my baby, and wrapped the blanket tightly about us. The others had all been startled too, and I knew they were awake so I hoarsely whispered, "What in the world was that?" The men said they didn't know, but Ross said his guess was that it was some kind of owl. I had heard owls back home, but none of them sounded anything like that, so I was still very frightened. The baby was madly voicing his disapproval of being so suddenly awakened, and my nerves were screaming to high heaven. To keep from crying, I made myself silently angry and lay down again, fairly seething with indignation at camping trips and foolish people who indulge in them and reciting all the indignities that I had been subjected to on this trip. Finally, I calmed down to the extent of being drowsy when that damned bird let out another of his confounded screeches, and I was breathless with fright all over again. What a night that was! I managed after a while to squelch my fear enough to get in a bit more sleep before morning.

Again we were up before dawn cooking breakfast by lantern light. Thank goodness the bugs weren't as bad in the morning. Daylight found the men on their way onto the lake to set more nets and take the fish from those they had set the day before.

Mrs. Bodi and I busied ourselves making a few improvements to our crude camp. The men wouldn't be back before 3 o'clock, so there was nothing to do but sit around on our uncomfortable boxes and for me to take care of the baby. I could see this same monotonous grind stretching ahead of me day after weary day for the duration of our stay.

Campfires and Indians

When the men came in from the lake, there was a lot of excited talking and gestures. When they got ashore, they told us that a boat had come up to them out in the lake, and the men on board said they had just come from the dredge that was digging the Lauderdale Canal. The body of a Seminole Indian, DeSoto Tiger, who had been trapping in the Everglades with a certain John Ashley had been found floating in the canal. He had been shot between the eyes. The officers from Palm Beach and Dade counties, as well as the US Marshall from Miami, were hunting for Ashley.

Good heavens, I thought, this outlaw stuff really is true, and here we are right in the middle of this swampy wilderness. I imagined all sorts of things happening to us if John Ashley should come our way. Mrs. Doss had been keeping close to her own tent and we hadn't met her, but this excitement brought her out where the rest of us were, and we were introduced to her. She was French and spoke very little English so kept to herself most of the time and was no company at all.

We all realized that this murder of an Indian by a white man was serious business and was something for the federal authorities to handle. To us, who came from a settled country where murder was unheard of, it was enough to send us back where we came from, if we had had the price of tickets. But, since we didn't, I just sat chewing my fingernails and made up my mind to stay it out.

In front of Dad's shack on the creek bank was what must have been the remnants of an old Indian camp. A half dozen long poles set in the ground, three on each side to support small poles fastened across the tops of these and a thatched roof of palmetto fans laid over all. The four sides were left open. (The palmetto fans had to be brought in by boat since there were no palm trees on the island.) This shelter made a nice place for a campfire around which to gather in the evening, so on the evening after we learned of the murder of DeSoto Tiger, Dad gathered wood and we had a campfire with everybody gathered around except Mrs. Doss, who had retreated once again to her tent.

We had company too that evening. A crew of fishermen who were camped on Little Kreamer Island just north of Torry came and spent a few hours with us around the campfire and discussed "the killin." They also gave hair-raising descriptions of other gruesome happenings in the Everglades.

Another evening as we were seated round the campfire, a man who had been hunting alligators for their hides and trapping raccoons and otters down in the Everglades came in to share our fire and camp for the night. He turned out to be quite entertaining and told the weirdest tale about having camped on an Indian mound on the Democrat River for the past few nights. He vowed that every night at about 2 or 3 o'clock in the morning he was awakened by the strangest music that came right out of that Indian mound. We were mesmerized by this tale, although we took it all with a grain of salt.

The next day I asked Dad if there was such a place as that, and he assured me that there was. Naturally, we were all interested and decided we would have to see it since it wasn't so very far away. On Sunday after the boat returned from Fort Myers, we all made the trip over to the mainland and up the Democrat River for half a mile or so and, sure enough, not one but two mounds were there. The larger mound was perhaps three times as large as the smaller one, the larger being about 12 or 15 feet higher than the surrounding soil level. These mounds were built entirely of sand that had been hauled in by boat from some place, perhaps the north end of the lake, which is sandy. All of the soil around the south end of the lake and on the islands is all black muck except for a bit on the north shore of Kreamer Island.

On the large mound was a huge lime tree full of limes, and on the smaller mound grew a grapefruit tree that was full of fruit. (The Smithsonian Institute did some excavating in these mounds in 1932-1933.) It had been a very pleasant trip for a Sunday afternoon. We all knew that these mounds were burial grounds, but who could say how many canoe loads of sand it took to build them. As for the music that the 'gator hunter said he had heard, well, we just left that to him and his fancies.

After a while, an elderly man in the visiting crew decided it was time for some music, so he started to play. From where I sat, I couldn't see the man plainly, and for the life of me, couldn't tell what sort of instrument he was playing. Whatever it was, it made good listening. Dad finally moved over near me and asked me how I liked the music. I told him it was very nice indeed, but asked, "What in the world is he playing?" "Just his nose," said Dad.

It was surprising to hear such sounds coming from a nose that was being pinched, pulled, and pushed around. The only sounds I had ever heard coming from a nose being treated like that were annoying instead of pleasing. Only one other time have I heard a "musical nose" (that is actually what they call them). That was at a parent-teacher reception in Canal Point some 20 years later, only that nose had to have piano accompaniment.

The nose finally got tired and the crowd began to scatter. It had been a hard day, and we were all glad to get into bed. Those cursed owls must have been protesting against those white tents in the clearing because they perched on the trees near us and screeched away night after night. I couldn't get a decent night's sleep no matter how I tried. I never did get over being startled by their dreadful cries.

Cut Off From Civilization

Next morning the captain of the Mabel told the ladies to make a list of groceries and things we would need because he would finish getting his boat load of fish that morning and expected to leave for Fort Myers right after noon. I had never been on a camping trip before, not even for a day, to say nothing of a night, so this undertaking was entirely foreign to me. Up to now Ross, who had spent most of his summers camping and knew about such things, had managed all the details of getting and packing the equipment and the first lot of groceries. Now, with Ross fishing on the lake, it was up to me. Not knowing what was expected, I was at my wit's end, so I turned to Dad, bless his heart. I don't know how I would have managed without him.

Dad told me that the boat would be gone for 5 or 6 days, and it was wise to always keep plenty of canned stuff and flour and shortening on hand so if the boat were to break down and not get back in time, we wouldn't be without something to eat. The captain took with him the lists we each wrote of our grocery and other needs.

bought the things, and brought them to us on the return trip.

Until then, I hadn't given the business of getting groceries the first thought. All of my life I had lived where we could get to a grocery store in a short time, and it hadn't occurred to me that there was no place nearer than Fort Myers to get groceries. It was frightening to realize what a puny thing was the chain that linked us to the grocery store. It would be anything but funny if the boat were to break down or be held up in some manner and us with no food. So I set about making my list, which turned out to be quite long, and had it ready for the captain when he came for it.

With a heavy heart I watched the boat leave us behind on Torry Island that afternoon. As she pointed her nose into the west headed for Fort Myers, I realized that the only connecting link we had with the outside world was gone. I began counting on my fingers the days she would be away and when she was expected to return.

Back in those days, Florida wasn't as well known and talked about as it is today. Consequently, I knew very little about it and knew nothing whatsoever about Lake Okeechobee and the Everglades. As a child, I had read a couple of stories about the floating islands in Lake Okeechobee, which were so fantastic I didn't get any sense out of them, so I began asking questions. Dad and Ed, being the only Floridians in the camp, were a willing source of information. Sitting around the campfire in the evenings, they told us about the Everglades and the plan to drain them, which was then being put into operation. Three canals were being dug from the lake to the Atlantic Ocean. One would connect with the Miami River at Miami, one with the North New River at Fort Lauderdale, and the other with the Hillsborough River at Deerfield.

The only route from the lake besides the way we came was up the Kissimmee River to Kissimmee. That trip was much longer than to Fort Myers. The river was almost impassable. It was expected that the canal to Fort Lauderdale would be cut through to the lake before the year was out and the distance from Torry Island to Fort Lauderdale would be about 65 miles, which was about half the distance to Fort Myers. Dad's home was at Pompano, so he was very anxious to see the canal to Fort Lauderdale put into use, since Pompano is just a short distance from Fort Lauderdale.

In the days while the boat was away at Fort Myers, the men finished setting their nets and had put up our tents, built the floor in the sleeping tent, and built a couple of crude beds and a table. So now we were set up in fine style, and at last there was some place to put the baby down where he could creep about and play.

Camp Life

Camp life soon became very monotonous. The men were out in the lake at their fishing all day, and for Mrs. Bodi and me, the few camp chores were soon attended to. The daily wash for the baby was always on the line early, so the days stretched out seemingly endlessly. I had brought needlework and crocheting with me and occupied myself in that way, but Mrs. Bodi had not provided herself with any of these things, and it wasn't many days before she was loosening that sharp tongue of hers. She certainly made life miserable for the baby and me. I soon found myself keeping the baby where I could keep an eye on both him and her constantly, since I realized she didn't like children. I was afraid of what she might do to him were she given an opportunity.

One day while the baby was playing in the tub set out in the sunshine, he fell and bumped his mouth on the edge of the tub, cutting his lips quite badly with his teeth. The blood spurted out, and the front of his dress was soon covered with it. This, with his screaming and crying, had me quite beside myself. The men were all out in the lake, so I had no one to turn to for help but her. Instead of her doing anything to help me, she just laughed. After this I was sure she must be a heartless fiend to have no feeling for a baby hurt like that, so I spent most of my spare time sitting under Dad's thatched roof, which made her more sullen and angry than ever. Several days after the baby's accident, Dad's son Ed had the misfortune to cut his hand quite badly while dressing fish. Before leaving Toledo I had stocked quite an emergency kit, so I got out disinfectants, salve, and bandages and cleaned and dressed the injured hand. This simple act of kindness brought forth from her the most violent tirade against me that I have ever heard. For some unknown reason, she seemed irate that I had bothered to help poor Ed with his injured hand.

When Ross came home, I managed to get him out of hearing of the others and told him what had happened and that I simply could not put up with that woman one minute longer than I had to and I would be very pleased if we could move our tents off to ourselves. He agreed that it was a bad situation for the baby and me and would do something about it soon.

On the opposite side of the creek down nearer the lake was a clump of likely looking shade trees, and we decided we would clear up a place there and move our tents as soon as possible. In a few days the lake was too rough for fishing, so work on the clearing started. By the time the weather had settled so the fishing could be resumed, our clearing was in shape to receive our tents, but now Ross would have to attend to the fishing and get the boat loaded and on its way back to town first.

This had been the first spell of rough weather we had, so the men were rather worried about their nets. Sometimes in stormy weather the weeds that grow in the lake would become so entangled in the nets they would roll up in a huge rope and often would have to be brought ashore, cleaned of weeds and trash, then reset. This time the men were fortunate in that respect. The nets had collected very little debris, but from one net they took an 8-foot alligator. Usually a gator would get into a net, eat all the fish he wanted, and then tear his way out, leaving a huge hole in the net. This would have to be mended before the net could catch fish again. This gator must have been lazy because he hadn't damaged the net. They caught him, trussed him up with ropes, and brought him in to camp alive.

We had a big campfire that night, and everyone turned out to see the alligator because none of us in the camp except Dad and Ed had ever seen one before. The mouth of the 'gator had been tied shut and the feet tied to the body so he couldn't bite or crawl away. I didn't get very close to the ugly thing myself. He looked too bad to me, but all the rest squatted around close by, and Ross even let the baby walk up and down the rough back a couple of times. I soon decided I had enough of that reptile, so took my baby and myself off to bed. The others stayed on around the fire and talked and listened to alligator stories told by Dad and Ed. Henry Bodi was standing beside the gator with one foot resting on its back when the thing evidently got tired of such goings on, flopped that tail around like a whip lash, knocked Henry's foot out from under him, and slapped him several feet away, almost landing him in the creek. This caused quite a commotion, and the folks faded back away from that 'gator like magic. Henry picked himself up, brushed away at the dirt on his clothes, looked around at the 'gator and said, "That damn thing liked to got me; nearly broke my leg, he did!" This, of course, broke the tension and everyone laughed. Interest in the 'gator was a thing of the past, and the men decided it was bedtime anyway, so each hurried himself off to his bed. Henry, though, nursed a lame leg for several days after. Next morning Dad and Ed skinned the gator, salted the hide, and sent it to Fort Myers to be sold. Alligator hides brought a pretty fair price those days, and there were quite a number of men who did nothing but hunt gators and sell the hides for a living.

3

Mother Nature at Her Best

A Permanent Home

In due course, the boat was on its way back to Fort Myers, and we set about building a floor and getting our tent and belongings moved. We were finally settled in our own little clearing on my birthday, February 7th, and, although we had no idea of it at the time, this was to be our permanent home.

Our tent was not very large, only 10 feet wide by 12 feet long. With a bed, trunk, table, stove, and cupboard of sorts, it was pretty well filled up, but it seemed like heaven to me to be away from that frightening woman and to have things a bit our own way for a change.

On inspecting our surroundings, I noticed a plot at the edge of our clearing that could easily be cleared. I called Ross's attention to this and said it would make a fine garden spot. "Garden spot!" said Dad and Ed. "Why, it's all muck. You couldn't raise anything in that. You have to have sand land for farming." I said, "Well, where I come from, we have a lot of black muck, and we farm it up there, so I'm going to plant a garden here, and I'll bet you will help eat the vegetables, too." So we set to work at our clearing using the logs and brush to make a fence to keep out the wild hogs. By the time the boat made another trip and brought back the seed, we had quite a garden spot ready. I planted the usual garden seeds and had quite a strip of land left over, so I saved the eyes from the potatoes we used and planted them there. In no time at all the garden was up and growing fine, much to the amazement of Dad and Ed. When other Crackers heard about my garden, they too came to see it and to marvel at things growing in that black dirt where there wasn't a bit of sand. This was the first garden stuff to be raised in what is now known as the winter vegetable basket.

Alligators and Other Critters

One day soon after moving to our new location, Ross said, "Come on, it's time you got a look at the lake. I want to show you something." All curious about what it was all about, I brought the baby and went out in the boat with him. When we got out where the creek opened into the lake, there were high rushes on either side of the channel. Lying on beds of matted reeds sunning themselves were several of the largest black water snakes I have ever seen. There was a light breeze from the east that drifted us slowly along. Suddenly Ross put an oar down and stopped the boat. He whispered, "Look." Looking in the direction he indicated, I saw one of these snakes in the process of making his bed of reeds. He would swim around getting into the proper place and position, then rear his head up and wrap himself partially around a reed and break it down on the place where the bed was to be. We watched for quite some time while the snake industriously worked away. Even though I was frightened of those huge snakes, it was fascinating to watch. However, I was very glad when we moved on because my mind was full of all sorts of dreadful things that could happen if one of those snakes ever decided to wrap its slimy self around me. I was much relieved later in the day when Dad told me that those snakes lived in the water and he had never seen one on land.

Dad also told us that alligators built their nests in the water much the same, only using their tails and mouth to do their construction work. The alligator builds her nest in a mound higher above the water to keep the eggs dry. On the top of the mound, she makes a depression where she lays the eggs and then goes on about her business while the sun hatches the eggs. The mother gator hangs around her nest and, when the eggs hatch, watches over the little ones. She has a peculiar grunt with which she calls the little ones to her. This grunt is easily imitated by people and was often used to call up the little ones so they could be caught alive.

Dad also said that now that spring was here it was mating time for the gators, and if we listened just before dawn, we would be hearing the gators lowing. He said he had heard one the previous morning over on the east side of the island and, from the sound of it, it must have been a big one. How odd, I thought, to speak of alligators lowing. We listened and sure enough a few mornings later we heard it. It seemed the island fairly shook from that rumbling bellow. Lowing was surely the right word.

The things that gave me goose bumps and cold chills most often were the huge tree spiders, blue lizards, and scorpions. The spiders were unbelievably large. I saw many of them that must have measured 5 inches from tip to tip of their legs, and the webs were strong enough to entangle and hold small birds. When one of them ran across the roof of the tent, it sounded like a rat running. The spiders weren't bad about coming inside, but the blue lizards were always scurrying around inside the tent. When I brushed at them with the broom, their tails would fall off and lie wriggling on the floor. Some of the old timers said they were poison, but others said no; so we didn't know what to believe, but we were desperately trying not to take any chances. We never went to bed at night without first taking all of the covers off the bed and looking under the mattress to make sure there were no snakes or lizards coiled up in the springs and no spiders among the blankets and pillows.

Breaking Camp

About the first of March, all of the folks who were camped in Dad's clearing broke camp and went back to Ohio and Michigan. We talked of going with them, but Ross didn't seem very anxious to go so soon, so I told him that if he wanted to stay until later in the spring I would stay with him. Besides, my garden was just beginning to ripen, and I was anxious to see how the beans and potatoes turned out. So, we decided to stay until May.

It truly seemed lonesome with only Dad and Ed left to talk to. I often went out to the trot line with Ross. I would put the baby in a tub set in the boat, and I cut the bait while Ross baited the hooks and took off the fish. One day when I hadn't gone with him, Ross came in from his fishing and said a man named Mr. Waggoner had come to him out in the lake and told him that he and his family lived on Kreamer Island and would like for us to come to see them. I was anxious for some other company, so I readily agreed.

Kreamer Island

Kreamer Island lies to the north of Torry Island and Little Kreamer Islands It was about a 3-mile row to get to the man's place; so the first slack day we set out to see if we could find the place and to see what Kreamer Island had to offer.

Our fishing grounds lay mostly to the south from the creek, and I had never before been to the north. For perhaps a fourth of a mile out from the shore of the islands grew various kinds of grasses, rushes, and weeds of different kinds that grew under the water on the lake bottom. Water lilies and water hyacinths grew in profusion and were in full bloom, a veritable riot of color all along the shore. This afforded a haven for wild ducks and coots (which were plentiful), but we had no shotgun.

After about 3 miles of rowing, Ross recognized the landmarks that had been described to him. We were soon teetering our way to shore on what seemed to be a very insecure landing walkway, just a few stakes driven down into the soft mud with cross pieces nailed to the tops and a single plank laid on this. The stakes weren't very close together, so the planks at the center would bend way down so that on the first half of the plank one seemed to be going down grade, while on the last half, it was up hill, while the entire structure swayed sideways, enough to make one seasick.

We managed to get to shore without mishap and started up a narrow footpath overgrown on either side with weeds about knee high. About 200 feet up from the dock, the path wound around a heavy clump of custard apple trees and opened into the clearing where the house stood. It is impossible to describe the feeling that came over me when I looked upon that place. I couldn't imagine any man, no matter how poor he might be, allowing his family to live in such squalor.

This family consisted of the father, mother, and 8 children: the eldest was a girl of 16 named Edith and youngest was a 2-year-old baby. The house, if one could call it that, was not much larger than our tent. There were no windows in the house, just an opening on either side with burlap sacks nailed at the top; these were tied up in good weather and let down when it rained. Overhead a few boards were laid across the ceiling joist and beds were laid on these boards. The beds consisted of burlap sacks sewn together to make a large sack the size of a mattress and was stuffed with wild grass. At one side of the house a few pieces of corrugated roofing tin were put up for a shelter for a tiny cook stove, and around the sides, the boards from grocery boxes and crates were nailed.

The two smallest children were digging in the muck near the door, and when they saw us, they scampered inside. The mother met us at the door and asked us in. There were no chairs, just boxes and hampers for seats. It was dreadfully hot inside, and I was glad indeed when introductions were over and she suggested that we sit out under the trees.

The man of the family had left that morning with a load of fish to go to Fort Myers. He owned his own boat and fished several nets. Some of the children, including 16-year-old Edith, her 14-year-old sister Mabel, and her 13- and 12-year-old brothers, were his crew and helped with lifting the nets and dressing the fish. Fishing was good. They should have been making lots of money, yet they lived like this.

They were all very friendly and talkative. At first, they all tried to talk at the same time and kept their eyes pinned on me, which was quite embarrassing. Finally, the mother said, "Mrs. Winne, you are the first white woman we have seen in eighteen months. That's how long we have been here." I was aghast. Here was this father with his own boat making regular trips to Fort Myers who kept his wife and children in this wilderness, never being taken on a trip with him in all that time. It was hard to believe. I asked her if she didn't think the children should be in school. She said she certainly did think so. Her husband was a college graduate, and when he talked her into coming to the island, he said he would build a nice five-room house for them and set up a place and teach the children himself. He had brought enough material to build the house, but the tiny shack was all he ever built. The rest of the lumber lay rotting in the edge of the clearing. The children's lessons had never been started. The two oldest girls could read and write, but the other children couldn't even read their own names. The sun was getting low, and it was time for us to start back to our own island. They all walked with us down to the dock and kept calling to us as we rowed away as though reluctant to see us leave. We promised to come back again before going back north.

On the north end of Kreamer Island, a long, narrow spit of sand jutted out to the northwest. Snow white birds kept raising up over this, flying a short way, then settling down again until finally the air was filled with white birds flying out a little way over the water, then back again, and never getting very far away. When a bird strayed off a bit from the flock, we could see what appeared to be a very long tail, so we guessed that they were plume birds or egrets. We made a mental note to ask Dad about them when we saw him.

The next day the weather was stormy, so we rowed up the creek to pay Dad and Ed a visit and to ask about the birds. Dad told us that the birds were egrets. The government protected these birds, and if anyone was caught with one of the plumes in his possession, it cost him a heavy fine. He said that despite that, men made a business of killing these birds for the plume and bootlegged them in the various tourist towns on the coast.

These birds have unusual habits. When they lay their eggs, they have a common nest and all lay in the same place, covering the entire ground with eggs. The plume grows out of the back, just behind the wings. By the time the birds have finished laying their eggs, the plume is fully grown. Then all the birds sit over the eggs and the plume helps cover them. So the plume has a practical purpose other than being beautiful. After the eggs are hatched, the birds shed the plume.

When hunters are after egrets, they go to a likely place and watch to see where the birds fly up from their nest. (These nests are called rookeries.) Then they sneak up on the place and shoot the birds while they are sitting on the eggs, thus not only killing the mother birds but all of the unhatched young. When the plume is taken from the bird, it is skinned off the back with a patch of skin about the size of the palm of the hand. All of the fat is carefully removed. Then while still fresh, it is smoothed out and placed on a piece of this porous paper to which it adheres and which holds it in shape It is then placed in the shade to dry.

About two weeks after our trip to Kreamer Island, a plume hunter camped overnight at our place. He had two suitcases full of plumes and was making his way to Miami to dispose of them. He showed us the plumes, but to me, though they were beautiful, I would never care to own one after learning how the birds were slaughtered to obtain them.

Spring on Torry Island

April was well on its way when we decided it was about time again to break the monotony of camp life, so we settled for a trip all around Torry Island. One nice morning I packed a picnic lunch and off we went exploring.

Our only means of travel was by rowboat, so we lazily rowed north, then through the pass between Torry Island and Little Kreamer Island, then south down the east side of the island. The shallow water here seemed like a fairyland. There were water lilies of every color: white, yellow, orchid, and an odd bluish one not as plentiful as the others. There were tall yellow chinquapins, blue and yellow flag, and purple hyacinths everywhere, while on shore forming a backdrop for all this were the custard apple trees draped with moon vines and wild asters. Nestled in this environ were tree orchids and air plants in bloom, and on the ground were giant wild ferns stretching up its tall graceful fronds.

About midway down the island, a huge flock of curlew arose from somewhere on the island, circled and darted about overhead. In the flock was one pink one, the first pink curlew we had ever seen. The pink was so bright it looked as if it must have been dipped in dye. It was beautiful to watch these birds. All were white with black wing tips except for this one of bright pink. In flight, it seemed as if they were trying to keep the pink one surrounded by the white ones all the time and never allowed it to get to the outer edge of the flock.

On nearing the south end of Torry Island, we saw a huge alligator. We always liked to think it was the one who shook the island with his lowing early in the mornings. He lay on a small mound of earth, lazily sunning himself and didn't even move as we rowed by not more than 50 feet away. Ross said he must have been 14 or 15 feet long. In all my years in Florida, I have never seen another gator as large as that one.

The sun was getting low in the west when we rounded the southern tip of the island and headed our boat north up through the familiar fishing grounds on to our creek and the little tent in the clearing. It had been a lovely day and a wonderful trip with Mother Nature at her best. We tumbled into bed that night very tired, but with a feeling of contentment and well-being.

4

This Wild, Lonely, Beautiful Place

Homesteading

Now began the serious thinking and talking about returning to Ohio. We couldn't make up our minds about when we should break camp and go. Fishing was good and the weather ideal.

During the interim, Mr. Waggoner, our neighbor from Kreamer Island, paid us a call. He was greatly interested in the remnants of my garden and asked a lot of questions about what we had planted, how it grew, was it good or poor quality, what about the flavor, etc., etc., until I finally asked him why he had never tried gardening since he was so interested in it. He answered that he had always wanted to try but had never had the time. He said his main reason for establishing his family on Kreamer Island was that he hoped some day the islands would be declared homestead lands, and he wanted to enter a claim if and when they were.

We hadn't given any thought to such possibilities. The only thing we had been interested in was a place to camp and fish during the winter; however, the man gave us a lot of food for thought. He told us that the islands in the south end of the lake had never been surveyed. He was in hopes that we would make up our minds to stay and stake out a tentative claim on Torry Island as he planned to do on Kreamer. There was another island about 7 miles to the west of Torry named Ritta, and a few families had recently come there to camp. He hoped to see those people in a few days, and if he could induce them to settle on that island, we could all get together and petition the government to have these islands surveyed while the government engineers were still here in the Everglades. Then, if the islands were surveyed, we would again petition the government, asking that the islands be declared homestead lands.

These islands were the only high, dry land anywhere in the south end of the lake. The rim of the lake from Bacon Point on the east side of the lake down around the south end and up the west side of the lake to Sand Point (now Clewiston) was all under water anywhere from 6 inches to 3 feet deep. At Sand Point was a high ridge tapering southward to Bare Beach; north again from Sand Point to Fisheating Creek was all underwater. So the only land high and dry enough to live on were these islands. The Bolls Company, who owned a large acreage of Everglades, had built a small hotel where the canal from Miami was to open into the lake. This hotel was built over the water, and boats were tied to the doorsteps here too. This hotel was built in anticipation of the Everglades being drained and was to be used to house prospective land buyers. (The engineers surveying the Everglades used a contraption they called a "go devil." This was a barge-like vehicle with caterpillar-like things on either side, which propelled it across the swamps, water, and mud alike.)

Mr. Waggoner left us, saying he expected to come back to see us in a week or 10 days to let us know about the decision of the people on Ritta Island. After he was gone, we were very quiet, each thinking our own thoughts for a long time. I knew that Ross would never ask me to stay on in this wild, lonely, beautiful place. If we stayed, the decision would have to be mine. It seemed to me that the weight of the whole world had suddenly been dumped onto my shoulders.

I finally decided that I would not bring the subject up for any discussion until we again heard from Mr. Waggoner. It could be that the people on the other island wouldn't or couldn't stay on, and then the whole idea might fall through. In the meantime, I would try to list the pros and cons of staying on Torry Island and get them all carefully catalogued in my mind so as to prepare myself for a sensible discussion when the time came.

Those were terrible days. At times I was sure that I could never bear the loneliness and isolation permanently. We had been on the island for more than 3 months now, and neither of us had been any farther away than to Kreamer Island. There just wasn't any place to go. No neighbors, no amusement of any kind. The only diversion was going out in the boat. I had never cared much for boats in the first place, and I was beginning to detest them.

We hadn't brought much clothing with us, and our wardrobes were sadly in need of replenishing. Besides that, what about the baby? He was a healthy, happy youngster, and I had always been handy about caring for babies so I wasn't worried about the usual baby fussiness. But what if he were really to get sick? That thought frightened me for days. Then I though, "How foolish! Here in this good clean air, he stands a better chance of staying well and healthy here than anywhere else."

I had to admit that the place had grown on me. Our little grove was quite attractive now. We had cleared away all the underbrush and planted a few wild climbing asters that were now in full bloom. We had transplanted air plants among the branches of our own grove of trees and around the outer edge of our clearing, the moon vines had draped over the custard apple trees and hung clear to the ground, forming a dense green curtain to shut out the untidiness of the woods beyond.

We had a hammock made of barrel staves swung between two trees, where it was in the shade all day long. Between two other trees, we had built a comfortable seat, again using barrel staves. (We got our flour those days in wooden half-barrels.) On a tree near the front of the tent, we had nailed a box covered with oilcloth with an end hanging down over the front of the box fastened at the bottom to keep out the rain. In the back of the box we hung a mirror and on the bottom, which formed a shelf, we kept our toilet articles. Below this box at a convenient height, we had nailed another box to hold a bucket of water and washbasin, all very neat and convenient. We also had a small table outside where we often ate our meals. After 5 or 6 days had elapsed, I caught myself envisioning a little house in our clearing and, in a few years, a real farm around it. Then I would realize how impossible it was for us to even think of staying with a youngster who would one day have to go to school and, of course, there couldn't possibly be a school here.

So, day after day passed and I couldn't come to a decision. Then Mr. Waggoner again came to see us. He had been to Ritta Island and had found four families there. They, all being Floridians, had great faith in the country and the possibilities of development so had readily agreed to stay on and make a try at the homesteading plan.

When Mr. Waggoner finished telling us this, Ross gave me a long, significant look, and that was all. He still wasn't saying a word, but I knew from that look that he wanted very much to stay and hoped that I wanted to stay too. It was for me to decide, and I would get no help from him. No one will ever know how awful I felt to have to make this decision all by myself. Here we were, two young people with our future stretching out before us, a baby to raise, and everything seemed to be standing still, waiting for my yes or no.

There was nothing for us to go back to in Ohio except our relatives and the familiar surroundings. Our fishing business had been wiped out in a bad blow the fall before, so if we went back we would have to start all over again. It was the wrong time of year for that, so staying where we were seemed the only sensible thing to do. Therefore, I finally forced myself to say, "Well, if you will build us a little house so we can get inside and shut out the things that frighten me so, I'll do my best to put aside my loneliness and we can stay until next year. Then we can truly decide if we will stay longer or if we will leave."

No amount of imagination can ever tell you about the flip-flops my heart was doing or about how a knife-like pain stabbed through me as I made that announcement and committed myself to a whole year of nothing, just loneliness and more of it as the days went by. I often wondered whatever possessed me to do it. Then I would remember that look on Ross's face and realized there was nothing else for me to do. So it was settled for a time and, in a way, it was a relief. It's pretty awful to just live from day to day with no plan for the future, however small that plan may be. It's still something to work for.

When Mr. Waggoner left that day, he said that when we got ready to build our house he would gladly help us to get the foundation squared up and started and would cut a pattern for the rafters. Ross greeted this offer with enthusiasm, because as he acknowledged, as a carpenter he was a good fisherman. Before night came, we had decided to put the house just in front of the tent. We would have to cut down one of our nice trees, but the spot was ideal for the house. We had put the tent about 150 feet from the creek and that was quite a distance to carry water, as the creek was the source of supply. Using the size of our tent as a gauge, we decided that our house would have to be 14 by 16 feet. We would use 10-foot sidewalls and make the ceiling downstairs about 7 feet high. This would give us about 2½ feet on the sidewall upstairs, and this plus the peak would make an ideal sleeping place. Since the boats that carried the fish weren't built to handle lumber, we knew it would take several trips for them to bring in enough lumber for even so small a house, but after that tent, it would seem like a mansion.

This called for a trip to Fort Myers to place an order for lumber and arrange how it was to be sent. Also, it was time we had a little settlement with the company that handled our fish. It now being the last of April, we decided on the middle of May for the trip. Until now, everything had been ideal. As far as weather conditions were concerned, the days were cool and pleasant with just an occasional shower. The mosquitoes were very few, the snakes had kept to themselves, the possums, coons, and wildcats hadn't given us any trouble, and even the owls had stopped screeching. All of these things must have been on their good behavior just waiting until we made up our minds to stay so they could really tear loose.

Sickness Comes to the Islands

A few days after Mr. Waggoner's visit as I was taking the wash from the line, a small motor boat pulled up to our landing and it was Mrs. Waggoner and the oldest girl. Mrs. W. came rushing up to me and said, "You've got to come, you've just got to come. I just talked with your husband out in the lake, and he said it was all right for you to come." I said, "Come where? What's the matter?" Said she, "My little girl is dying and you've just got to come." Of course I would go, but whatever she expected me to do for her dying child I couldn't imagine. I couldn't help wondering why she wasn't with the child herself instead of over here to get me when the girls could just as well have come by themselves.

I put a few clothes for the baby in a suitcase and went with them. The nearer we got to Kreamer Island, the more I realized how foolish it was for me to take my baby into a place of illness, so when we got to our destination, I let one of the girls keep my baby outside while I went in to have a look at the sick child. She was very sick, but the mother had no idea what was wrong. Mr. Waggoner had left for town the night before, and the child was sick then, but they figured not sick enough to take to a doctor. So now they were having a man from the camp on Little Kreamer take the little girl to Fort Myers. Mrs. Waggoner and the oldest girl, Edith, were going with her, and they wanted me to promise to stay with the other children until they came back. I told her I couldn't promise that because there was no telling how long she would have to be away but that Mr. Waggoner should be back in a few days and I would stay until he came. It gave me the creeps to think of sleeping in those beds and staying in that awful house. I felt much safer in my tent.

I made it through the first night uneventfully, but the next day the weather sought to provide me with another challenge. A twister came across the islands, and the rain was so heavy for a couple of hours that when it was over the Waggoner's house was drenched. We tried to keep the beds dry but were not very successful. We turned the wet sides of the so-called mattresses down and hoped that the dry sides would stay dry enough for us to sleep on, which they didn't.

As a result, I caught an awful cold. The next morning I told Mabel I would have to go home and see if the rain had harmed my own belongings.

It was a bright, sunny morning with not a cloud in the sky, so after hanging out the wet clothing and bedding, Mabel and I, with the two small children, got into the little launch and made our way to Torry Island. The storm had hit here too, and sure enough, things in my tent were a mess. Ross was at Dad's when the wind struck. The tent flap hadn't been fastened securely so had blown open and the rain blew all over the tent. Finally, one of the guy lines broke and the tent collapsed, turning over my makeshift cupboard. My few dishes were nearly all broken and groceries scattered on the floor in all of that water. It must have been an awful mess, but Ross had done a good job of cleaning up and getting the tent back up.

Our clean clothing was kept in an old fashioned metal-covered trunk with a rounded top, so everything in that was dry, but our bed and whatever clothing wasn't in the trunk were all wet. I immediately set to washing them in hopes of getting them dry before we went back to Kreamer Island. I managed to get everything washed and on the line to dry before noon. I fixed dinner for us all, and while we were eating, the rain came pouring down again without a bit of warning. One minute the sun was shining bright and the next came the rain, drenching all those clothes and bedclothes flapping dejectedly on the line. I certainly had no desire to go back to Kreamer Island that evening, but there was nothing else to do, so I instructed Ross to take the clothes in before night. The clothes that were dry he could chuck into the trunk. The others could be put into the tub to hang out again the next day. We went back to Kreamer Island expecting to find everything there sopping wet again, but to our surprise, it hadn't rained there and everything was nicely dried out.

Mr. Waggoner returned the next day. The little girl was better but had to remain in town another week. It turned out her illness was a case of locked bowels from eating too many guava seeds with no thought being given to elimination.

I was glad to get back to my own place again and was determined to try to fix things a bit more securely. When I got home, much to my surprise, I found the mattress out in the sun, the pillows and bedding on the clothesline, and Ross down on his knees busily scrubbing the floor. We managed to get the bedding and pillows fairly dried out before the rain came that day, but the mattress was still damp and heavy, so we conceived the idea of lighting the coal oil lantern and setting it under the bed. The heat from the lantern did wonders in drying it out, so we could again sleep on it in comfort.

Dad paid us a short call that evening to inquire about the sick child and to chat a bit. He allowed as how the rainy season sure had set in and from now on we must expect this sort of weather every day for quite a spell, as the season usually lasted well into July.

Alone on the Island

After Dad left us, we had quite a powwow about the proposed new house. After realizing the extent of these Florida rainy seasons, we decided we had better start building our house as soon as possible, so we figured to make the next trip in on the boat. The mosquitoes were becoming quite annoying after dark. Keeping mosquitoes out of a tent is next to impossible.

Then I began to worry about what would happen to our few belongings while we were away if another twister and rain such as the one we had just had should happen to strike again. The more I thought about it, the less I liked the idea of us both leaving. I could only imagine how awful it would be to come back and find what little we had all wet a ruined, so very bravely I said, "I think I'll stay here." "What?" Ross said, "All by yourself?" "Yes," I said, "Just the baby and me—nothing will hurt us, and Dad and Ed are near in case we need help."

Ross had to admit that it was a risky thing for us both to go away, but he certainly didn't like the idea of me staying by myself for a whole week. But, stay I did. The boat pulled out early one morning and the captain promised to hurry back just as soon as possible, so I felt that surely they would be back in 6 days at the most. How little did I know.

All that day I was buoyed up by the thought of how brave I was. I vowed I wouldn't allow myself to become frightened, no matter what. Brave thoughts they were, especially in daylight hours. The weather was gentle that day and things didn't seem so bad, but when the sun sank out of sight and darkness came, I began to feel that the woods were all closing in on me and I could scarcely breathe. The baby must have sensed my fear. Usually he was a good-natured little fellow and stuck to his regular habits, but this night he began to fret and whine. Then I really became frightened and worried. My tears fell along with his until finally we were both exhausted and slept.

Morning dawned bright and clear. After the daily wash was on the line, I decided it was a good time to get started on some sewing. My mother had sent a few pieces of material for the baby and me. I would have to sew them by hand, and it would take quite a good many stitches to make a dress for me, but that would be a good way to spend my time while the baby and I were alone.

I had just laid the pattern on the material when Dad came up the path and called to me. I went out to see what he wanted, and he said that he and Ed had to leave too. A man in a small motorboat had come in the night and brought word that Dad's daughter was very ill, so they were leaving at once.

Now I was really frightened. The only other person on the island was a slow-witted man at Dad's camp who had been fishing with them. This man lived with Dad and Ed Simmons and helped them around the camp. I could tell by his speech that he was mentally challenged and benefitted from the kindness shown to him by Dad. Dad and Ed would have taken him with them, but the boat was too small. As their boat pulled away from our landing, I knew the true meaning of that old phrase, "the depth of despair." I had hit the bottom of the pit.

I went back into the tent, thoughtfully folded my material and put it away, then gave myself over to some serious thinking. Here were my baby and I on this lonely island with only one other occupant, that slow-witted man. My imagination began to take hold of me, and I started to imagine any number of dreadful things that could happen if this man went completely mad. A tent would furnish no security at all should his thoughts turn to harming my baby or me. The only weapons of any kind that I had for protection were an ax and a butcher knife less than 8 inches long. These wouldn't be very effective in the hands of a woman against a crazy man. There wasn't a thing I could do but watch, wait, and pray.

To make things seem worse, the weather went on a rampage again that afternoon. The wind blew furiously and the rain came pouring down with my tent being lashed about. When that wet canvas was blown up then suddenly slapped down on the ridgepole, it sounded like the crack of a pistol. Soon the rain was coming through the tent like a sieve, and I was kept busy for the rest of the afternoon trying to keep my bed dry and the tent from blowing away at the same time. It was quite a job, but I did it. It must have been nearly midnight before I dared to unroll my bed, crawl into it, and try to get some sleep, and sleep I did. After that strenuous battle with the elements, I was completely worn out.

The next morning I was awakened by a voice outside calling, "Miss, oh, Miss." I called back, "Wait just a minute." Dressing as hurriedly as I could, I went outside and there stood the man from Dad's camp. I was startled, but strange to say, not frightened. He asked me how I had fared during the storm and I told him "all right." "How did you make out?" I asked. "Well," he drawled, "I'm all right, but some of the paper blew off the roof right over the grocery shelf and all of my flour got wet. I wondered if you managed to keep yours dry and could spare me a bit." I told him that I must have been lucky because I managed to keep my food dry. (I always bought my flour in a wooden half-barrel, and for added protection besides the wood cover, I kept the barrel under the table that was covered with an oilcloth carefully tacked down all around the edges.) I asked him to have a seat outside, and I would be glad if he would share my breakfast with me.

We ate our breakfast out under the trees with mosquitoes nipping at our ankles. After breakfast, I gave him a tin bucket full of flour and cautioned him to always keep the lid on. Then it couldn't possibly get wet. He thanked me for his breakfast and the flour and returned to Dad's place. Soon I heard him hammering away, nailing the paper back on the roof. He was always working away at little chores around Dad's camp. From this point on, he was always polite and cordial to Ross and me even though we never became truly friends. I realized that he was not violently insane, just slow in his thoughts and mental abilities. I respected Dad Simmons even more for his kindness to this man.

Two days had passed, and this was the beginning of the third. The time for the boat to be away was nearly half gone, and I felt that after going through all of this these past 2 days, it surely couldn't be any worse during the remaining days. The rest of this third day passed uneventfully. The rain, when it came, fell gently, the wind having spent its fury the afternoon before. I got my dress nicely started; all of the baby's laundry got dry for a change, and the tent dried out and didn't feel so damp and depressing. When night came, I actually went off to sleep without shivering and shaking with fear until I was worn out.

The next morning started out bright and sunny as all the others had, but the sunshine didn't last as long. The rain started gently at first and at noontime it was raining so hard one could scarcely see through it. The trees were just a gray mass. Fortunately, there was very little wind and the rain didn't come through the tent, but I was ready for it if it did with the bed rolled up and covered snugly and all of the groceries covered tight.

About two o'clock that afternoon, the rain suddenly stopped. One minute it was furiously pelting the earth, the next minute it was stopped and soon the sun was shining. I decided that now would be a good time to catch up with some letter writing so as to have my letters ready for the boat when it came the day after tomorrow. The baby was having his afternoon nap, so I settled myself at the table and began to write. I do not know how long I had been sitting there lost in my letter writing when a slithering, scraping sound against the canvas aroused me. Glancing down at the tent flap opening, I saw a long, yellow snake crawling onto the floor. It was about half way inside and must have been all of 7 feet long.

Usually when I am badly frightened I become paralyzed and can't move, but fortunately not that time. The broom was within reach of my hand, and I grabbed it and brushed at the snake. Instead of the thing being scared and running out again, it struck at the broom. I kept brushing at the snake and it kept fighting back until I finally got the broom under the snake just right and pushed him off the floor to the outside of the tent. Before I could get outside and find something with which to kill him, he crawled under cover and got away from me.

After my fight with the snake, I became dreadfully ill and shook with one of the most violent chills I have ever had. I lay down beside my baby with my eyes glued to the opening in the tent, afraid to turn them away for fear that awful snake would come back again. I finally shook off the chill and set to work making the tent flap secure against snakes and crawling things for the night. I slept very little that night, getting up at every rustling noise or at the sound of a leaf scraping on the tent, feeling sure that it was another snake coming in.

What a relief a flashlight would have been, but there were no such things in those days, and I had to rely on matches and oil lamps and lanterns. To keep the matches dry enough so they would strike, we dried them out at the oil stove every day and kept them inside the closed trunk or in a pillow during the night. Even with these precautions, there were times when it was almost impossible to light a match. The match heads would become so softened from the dampness that they would just roll off the stick when we tried to strike them. We had no safety matches then, only those household matches in large boxes that weren't very good, even at their best.

Morning at last, and this was my fifth day alone on the island. With luck, the boat might come in tonight. If not, then surely it would be here early tomorrow. The day dragged by so dreadfully slowly. Some rain, some sun, plenty of cloudiness, but no boat. All through that night I strained my ears listening for the sound of motors that didn't come.

When morning came at last, it was such a bright, promising-looking day that I felt sure the boat would be coming along most any minute. I hurried through with the laundry and camp chores and baked fresh bread, a few cookies, and a pie, all in anticipation of the boat's return, bringing Ross back to me. Noon came and went, then evening, and finally night and still no boat. All through the night, the next day, and for days to come, I waited and listened and prayed.

The weather continued to act terribly, with rain and wind, mostly rain. One afternoon another twister hit and lashed things about unmercifully. The tree in front of the tent to which our toilet facilities were nailed was blown over and went crashing to the ground with a terrible noise. Fortunately, it fell away from the tent. Not long after the tree went down, one of the lines on the front corner of the tent gave way, and the tent was in danger of collapsing. I ran out into the storm to see what could be done. The line had chafed against something and was broken in two. I couldn't untie that wet rope to get line enough to tie it back together again. The rain was coming down in torrents, the wind was thrashing everything about like mad, and there I stood, holding to that line, being jerked about unmercifully while my baby was screaming at the top of his lungs inside the tent. I didn't dare let go for fear the whole thing would crash down on him. I looked about frantically hoping for a short bit of rope or trotline or something, just anything to fasten that damn thing back together again, when my eyes came to rest on a tub with some of the baby's clothes soaking in it. Thinking to myself, "Anything is worth a try," I took one of the diapers from the tub and tied it to the rope end on the tent, then, pulling it up as tightly as I could against that awful wind, I tied it fast to the other end of the rope. Then I went back inside the tent. I was thoroughly drenched, cold, and exhausted. The baby stopped his crying when I got inside where he could see me. I managed to get into some dry clothes and got into bed with the baby to try to get warm, though, chilled as I was, I was sure I never would be warm again.

And so the days went by until the 13th day. I was numb with worry and tired through and through from fighting the wind and rain, snakes, and fear, most of all fear, when about noon I heard the sound of motors. At first I was afraid to believe it, but kept listening and listening until I was sure the sound was coming nearer. Now that I knew the boat was really coming, I was half afraid to go out to meet it. I had been alone for so long and had gone through such ordeals as no lone woman should ever be called upon to face. I could only think of the number of dreadful things that could have happened to keep the boat away so long. I was in a good way to becoming panicky, but finally I forced myself to be calm and, taking up the baby, I walked down to our boat landing, arriving just as the boat came round a clump of reeds and headed up the creek. I can never describe the feeling that came over me when I saw that boat bringing people back into my life again after all of those dreadful days when I felt as though my baby and I were the only two people left in the world.

I stood there fully expecting the boat to stop at our landing. In the bow of the boat were Dad Simmons and Ed with a stranger. The Captain had his head out of the cabin window on one side and his partner on the other, but there was no sign of Ross anywhere. The boat kept coming on, not slowing down or anything, and finally went chugging on past. The men all lifted their hats to me as they went by and my heart did a terrible flop and landed at my feet. As if in a trance, I clutched the baby more closely, turned, and slowly walked back to the tent. Inside once more, I set the baby on the table, held him in the circle of my left arm while I sat myself down on an upturned hamper, laid my right arm across the table, dropped my head upon my arm, and burst into tears. I knew something dreadful had happened to Ross, and everyone was just putting off the ordeal of telling me.

I had been so sure that he would be on that boat when it came, and now the boat was here but no sign of him. It was too much for me. I just sat there sobbing my heart out and wondering whatever in this world I was going to do for I knew I could never stay another night in that place by myself. The more I tried to think, the harder I cried. When a hand fell on my shoulder and a voice spoke to me, I jumped up with the baby in my arms and backed away, screaming at the top of my lungs. I was so overwrought I couldn't recognize Ross, though I was staring right at him.

He realized that I was badly frightened and upset, in fact, on the verge of a nervous collapse, so he just stood there quietly until I finally came to my senses and recognized him. Then he spoke to me, but I, having run the gamut of my emotions, didn't even feel glad to see him. I had no feeling left for anything.

Ross took the baby from me, and I crumpled down on the bed and started sobbing bitterly and wildly all over again. It was quite some time before I calmed down enough to find out why I hadn't seen him on the boat. He had gone down into the cabin to get together his purchases of nails, hardware, and a few tools and had found that other things for Dad's camp had been piled on top of them. He was still busy inside the cabin as the boat went past our place. If I had stayed at the landing a minute longer, I would have seen him coming out of the cabin onto the stern deck. The boat had to unload a lot of stuff for Dad before they could unload our belongings, so they went on to his camp and Ross came back in a rowboat. Just as simple as that—for them—but oh, how terrible for me!

If I had declared then and there that I couldn't possibly stay any longer and wanted to go home, I'm sure Ross would have agreed that it was best that we should go, but such a thing never occurred to me. We had decided to stay for a year; that was that, and we would stay, no matter what.

The boat soon came back to our place to unload our bit of lumber and things. While Ross was looking after the unloading, I was cooking dinner. Then while we were eating, he told me what had happened on the trip. The two men who owned the boat had placed an order for a new motor several weeks before, and when they got to Fort Myers on this trip, the motor had arrived so the boat went on a ways for a motor change and general overhauling.

Then the men decided a paint job was necessary, which was more time consuming than anyone had expected, but there was no way of letting me know.

Ross made arrangements with the lumberyard for material for the house and outlined how it was to be sent. Since the boat could bring very little lumber at a time, it was imperative that as each lot of lumber arrived it should be built up before the next lot came. It all sounded so reasonable and simple that I felt silly for having worried and fretted myself into such a state. When I told Ross about the way I had spent the days while he was gone, I was ashamed to let him know how frightened and worried I had been. I tried to make the telling sound less awful. When I told him about the tent line breaking and how I had fixed it, I started to laugh, but wound up crying instead.

With a very serious, thoughtful look on his face, he went outside, untied the diaper from the tent line, spliced the rope, drew the corner of the tent back into place, and retied the line. Then he went all around the tent checking and tightening the lines and stakes, making sure that all were in good shape and that there was no danger of another line chafing in two.

Since there was still a few hours of daylight, Ross decided that he had better go out and see what shape his trotline was in and try to get it back to fishing again. He found his line badly twisted and tangled with weeds, so set to work straightening and baiting as much of it as he could. When he returned, he said he had more than half of it cleaned and baited for the night's fishing.

Next morning Ross was up and about before daylight, in a hurry to be out to his line to take off the fish he had caught during the night and to clear up the rest of his line and get it all to fishing again. A trotline is fished chiefly for catfish and consists of a running line of heavy maitre cord, usually nine-thread. This line is stretched between stakes that are set perhaps 100 feet apart, depending on how grassy the lake bottom might be. The hooks are tied to short lines that are called snoods. These snoods are tied to the running line just far enough apart so they cannot touch each other. At intervals of 15 or

18 feet, a float or cork is tied on to keep the line from sagging. For bait we used what is called "trash fish," such as mudfish, shad, and shiners, none of which were saleable. The bait fish were caught in a wire trap.

The catfish were kept alive in what was called a pound. It was made of wire mesh poultry netting nailed to a frame perhaps 8 or 10 feet square, which was set in the lake in some clump of rushes or other growth to protect it from rough water in case of a blow. When the boat came to the camp, the fish were taken from the pound, dressed, and iced down in the huge ice-box on the boat.

Ross returned about 10 o'clock having cleared up the remainder of his line and baited the whole length of it, about 500 or 600 hooks, which is quite a chore for one man to care for at any time. After lunch Dad Simmons and Ed came. They asked me when I had last seen the man they had left at their place when they went to Fort Myers, so I told them about his having come to borrow some food from me and that I had heard him hammering up there that day, but hadn't seen or heard him since. They told us that the fellow was gone, and from the looks of things around the place, he had been gone for some time but he had left his clothes. I told them I couldn't imagine where he had gone because there hadn't been any motorboats in the creek since they had been gone and all of the rowboats were accounted for. It was very puzzling. We talked of it and worried over it for several days when finally we got word that the man had managed to make his way through the dense growth and tangled mess of vines that covered the island, coming out on the north end of the island. He swam the pass over to Little Kreamer Island and was at a fish camp there. He refused to come back to Torry Island, said the place was haunted.

Building a Foundation

That afternoon Dad and Ed offered to help Ross get the house started, so they soon were busy cutting up the fallen tree and squaring up for the foundation. The foundation was the usual—posts driven into the ground, the tops squared off level, and then stringers nailed to them for the sills to rest on. When it was time for them to quit and go back out to their trotlines, the thing was beginning to look as if it would be a house someday, and I was feeling quite excited about it.

Now that Ross was home, the weather behaved in ordinary fashion for a couple of weeks—a bit of sun, a shower of rain, and very little wind. Each time the boat arrived, it brought more lumber and the house kept growing. Then the weather stopped behaving; the bottom seemed to drop out of the sky, and the rain poured down almost constantly. Whatever work was done had to be done when the rain slackened. Ross was soaking wet all day every day.

For 3 whole weeks we never saw the sun, and getting clothes dry was really a problem. I kept the oil stove burning constantly all through the day and had clothes hanging from the ridgepole all the time trying to get them dry. Most of the baby's clothes I baked dry in the oven. Sunny Florida, I thought, but where is the sun?

One day at the beginning of this intensely rainy 3 weeks, the run boat came in from Fort Myers about 8 o'clock in the morning with a larger amount of lumber than usual. About half an hour later a fishing crew, some half-dozen men from Ritta Island, tied up to our landing. They had learned from the captain of the run boat that we were building a house and that the lumber on board was for us, so they decided they would come over and give us a hand.

We did not know any of these men, had never even heard of them before, because they had only recently come to Ritta Island, but we were grateful for their offer of help. Dad and Ed had been helping Ross all along, and when all of those men set to work, they made a big showing. We had the usual amount of rain that day, but they all worked right through it.

I cooked dinner for them and had to feed them a few at a time because I didn't have enough dishes, pots, and pans to allow all of them to eat at the same time, but they seemed to enjoy it. They, as well as most fishing crews on the lake at that time, just "bached" and did their own cooking, so it was a treat for any of them to get a meal home cooked by a woman.

It was still early in the afternoon when they put up the last of the lumber that the boat had brought. While they worked at the house, I had busied myself making cookies and I served them coffee and cookies before they left for their camp. Two of those men remained on Ritta Island for several years, and we became good friends. The others we never saw again.

When the two by fours for the rafters arrived, Ross was really at a loss. He didn't know how to cut them. We got together and tried to remember how one was supposed to figure them out. We had both studied how it was done while we were in school, but couldn't remember the basic principles. Just as we were despairing, Mr. Waggoner came and cut one for us to use as a pattern. It looked so simple to see him do it, and he explained it all very carefully; but after he had gone we tried to work it out for ourselves, just to see if we could but had to give up in disgust and admit that we couldn't do it.

Mr. Waggoner's errand that day was to get us to sign the petition requesting the government to survey the islands in Lake Okeechobee, namely Ritta, Torry, Kreamer, and Little Kreamer. After Mr. Waggoner had gone, we discussed with the Simmons the possibility of the islands being surveyed anytime in the near future and whether the petition could possibly interest the "powers that be" in Washington.

Much was said, and the general opinion of the men was that this was just a pipe dream of Mr. Waggoner. They didn't expect anything to come of it, but I felt differently and said that inasmuch as the surveyors were already working in the Everglades, now was an opportune time to remind whoever was in charge of these things that the islands had never been surveyed, and if ever they intended to survey them, now was the best possible time. At any rate, we would just have to wait and see.

Anyway, my garden had proved itself and people on the islands were already talking of the gardens they were going to plant in the fall. They had helped to eat the lettuce, radishes, onions, cabbage, beans, and peas, all of which were now gone; we were beginning to scratch out a few new potatoes now and then. One morning we got up to find that some wild hogs had got into the garden during the night and had rooted the entire plot over. It looked as though it had been plowed, and all my lovely potatoes had been eaten. I could have cried.

A Visit from Captain Parker

Along about this time, we received word from a friend of Ross, an old deep sea captain, Captain Parker, telling us that he was captain on the drill barge that was working in the Lauderdale Canal, and he asked us to run down to see him. Dad and Ed had a small motorboat, so we talked with them about making a trip down the canal to see the captain. We planned that we would all go on the very first Sunday that the weather looked promising, so early one sunny Sunday morning I packed a picnic lunch and we started out. The boat was strictly a fishing tub, had neither speed nor comfort, and no canopy for protection from sun or weather; however, the weather was quite nice most of the morning as we monotonously chugged away. The mouth of the canal was about 4 miles from our landing, and when we entered the canal there was nothing to be seen but that endless ribbon of water with high muck banks on either side. There certainly was nothing exciting about that. This canal was being dug from both ends and when the dredges met, the canal would be cut through from the south end of the lake to Fort Lauderdale.

Late that morning we passed the place where the murdered Indian had been buried. A bleak marker gave the name "Desoto Tiger: Killed by John Ashley" and the date. To us this was a grim reminder that John Ashley was still at large, hiding somewhere in the Everglades. After the first excitement over this shooting had died down, we had put him out of our minds, so it was a bit of a shock to come so unexpectedly upon this lonely grave by the canal bank, with only miles and miles of water and saw grass all around.

When we came in sight of the dredge, the rain started, gently at first, then finally a downpour. What a mad scramble we had then One of the men was busy over the motor, trying to keep the spark plugs and wires dry, and the rest of us were madly bailing water out of the boat to keep it from swamping. We were all wet as drowned rats and must have been a sad-looking sight when we finally reached the dredge. The Captain invited us to come on board. We had no sooner clambered on deck than the rain stopped. I'm sure the good captain must have had a qualm or two about inviting us to come on board his nice clean dredge, but being a gentleman, he could scarcely do otherwise. He invited us to his cabin, showed us where to wash up, and of all things, a bathroom of sorts, very good sorts too, I must say, and plenty of soft bath towels.

I had learned a thing of two about the cantankerous Florida weather and had packed some things for the baby in a pail with a lid that set over the top on the outside, so I soon had him into dry clothes and I dried and combed my hair. By this time my clothing was drying out a bit, anyway it had stopped dripping, and, carefully holding the baby away from my damp clothes, I went back to the Captain's cabin.

When I came in, the Captain took the baby from me and talked and played with him and told us about his wife and children and how much he missed them and how lonely he got way out here so far from everything. It was nearing noon and the Captain invited us to have dinner with him and sent word down to the galley to lay plates for us.

When the dinner bell finally rang, the Captain carried the baby on his left arm, offered his right arm to me, and very graciously escorted us down to the dining room. As we were being seated, a couple of the men had no shirts on. The Captain gave them a look and a frown, and they disappeared to return almost at once with their shirts on.

I have often thought back on that visit with a great deal of pleasure. It was no novelty to Ross being on this dredge, as he had worked on boats and dredges and at fishing all of his life, but for me, this was the first time I have ever been on a dredge, and to find a Captain with drawing room manners and the quiet respectfulness of his rough-and-ready crew gave me a lot to think about as well as a great deal of pleasure. The Captain must have been a bit excited at having guests to dinner, as this one incident still stands out clearly in my mind. He had helped his plate to potatoes and picked up a pitcher with a ladle in it, presumably to put gravy on the potatoes, when the cook stepped up and said, "Oh, please, sir, no, Mr. Captain. That's the dressing for the pudding." The Captain grinned foolishly.

During our conversation, Ross had asked the Captain if he knew Captain Parker, and he said he had met him a few times. Ross then asked if he knew whether Captain Parker was on board the drill barge then. He said as far as he knew the Captain was on board, and he also said the drill barge was a short distance down the canal, so as soon as we decently could, we bade the Captain good day, thanked him for a pleasant time, and went chugging on our way down to the drill barge.

The sky was dark and threatening, and I was silently praying that the rain would hold off until we were on our way home because I didn't feel equal to being presented to any more strangers looking so limp and bedraggled. We soon reached the drill barge and were told that the Captain was on the houseboat because he was off duty, so we shoved off and made our way to the houseboat some half-mile away.

The Captain came out and invited us up on the small after-deck. He couldn't invite us inside because some of the crew was sleeping, while others were lounging around in curious stages of undress and, to quote him, "'Twas no place for a lady."

After visiting with the Captain for half an hour or so, we decided we had better get under way if we were to get home before dark. As we were leaving, the Captain said he would have a long weekend over July 4th, which was a couple of weeks away, and if his little motor boat didn't decide to lay down on the job, he would be up to look us over.

This drill barge performed the operation of drilling holes in the rocky bottom of the canal. Charges of dynamite were placed in these holes with the fuse attached to electric wires that were connected to batteries. At the end of each shift just before the crew went off duty and the fresh crew came to work, the drill barge was moved out of danger and the dynamite was discharged by flipping a switch on the battery. About two miles back from the drill barge was the dredge, busily engaged in taking the broken rock out of the canal and piling it on the bank. As we passed by the dredge on our way home, the Captain waved to us and asked us to come back again.

After about an hour had passed, the rain started again, and we had a miserable ride home as it continued to rain constantly. We arrived just before dark, tired and soaking wet, to find that a couple of wild hogs had managed to get into the tent and were making themselves at home. Thank goodness no damage was done other than mud all over the floor. We had long since learned to put the groceries up in tightly covered containers and pile everything up on the table.

The hogs scampered out without argument. I imagine they were as surprised to see us as we were to see them. We later learned how vicious some of those wild hogs could be, and we were indeed lucky that these weren't inclined to fight. While supper was cooking, I scrubbed the mud off the floor and got the baby ready for bed, and as soon as we had finished eating, we tumbled into bed.

Goodbye to the Waggoners

One afternoon a couple of days after our trip down the canal, Ross and Ed went out in the lake together to help each other move some of their trotlines to new fishing grounds. Ross said they would be a little late getting back so for me to fix a late supper for them. I knew from experience that this meant about nine o'clock, so cooked supper and had it ready at that time. Then I waited and waited, and they didn't come. I finally gave up trying to keep supper hot for them so turned the fire off and lay across the bed. About midnight they came, tired and hungry. As they were working on their last line, Mrs. Waggoner and one of the girls came to them, and Mrs. Waggoner told them that her baby was sick and asked Ross if I could come over. Our baby had caught a bit of a cold on Sunday, so Ross knew I wouldn't take him over there, so he and Ed said they would go over for a while and asked if there was anything they could do.

The baby had a bad case of croup, and Ross told Mrs. Waggoner she ought to try to get him to a doctor. Mr. Waggoner was in Fort Myers, so she thought she would wait until he came back. There was nothing the two men could do so they came on back home. A few days later Mr. Waggoner came home and the baby was much worse, so they left immediately for Fort Myers to try to get the little fellow to a doctor, but he died before they reached La Belle. They took him on to Fort Myers and buried him. Mrs. Waggoner refused to return to the lake any more.

They found a place for her and the children to live, then Mr. Waggoner returned to Kreamer Island, packed up their few bits of clothing, bundled all the rest of the children onto the boat, and moved them to town. He refused to support them, so they had to make their own way. About two years later, Mrs. Waggoner died and the children went to Michigan to live with relatives.

5

A Hard, Monotonous Grind

Company's Coming

During the latter part of June, Ross got a letter from his mother saying she and an older son, George, were planning to come to Florida in a few weeks. This was quite a bombshell. Our house couldn't be finished until the latter part of July, and there was no room in the tent to squeeze anyone else, or so I thought. I said, "Whatever will we do with them if they come?" and Ross said, "Write and tell them not to come until September." So I wrote the letter asking them to wait until September before coming down, explaining to them as best I could how little lumber the boat could bring in each trip and how long it was taking to build the house, how small the tent was, and how awful the mosquitoes had become. In fact, I mentioned everything I could think of to try to discourage them from coming until fall. Until the rains started we had no mosquitoes, but now they were terrible. At first they swarmed about only at night, and by getting inside and closing the tent tightly before dark, we managed to keep them out, but now we had to fight them all day long. I ordered a large piece of mosquito netting. When it came, we first cut an opening in the back of the tent for a window, leaving the top part of the canvas attached to the tent. We nailed a small strip of board across the bottom end and propped it up like an awning. When it would start to rain we could push the prop down from inside the tent and the canvas would fall back into place, thus keeping the rain out. Over the window I sewed a piece of netting. The rest of the netting I sewed across the top half of the front and down the corner. The net was long enough to lie on the floor, and we kept a board lying on this to hold it tightly to the floor. When the tent flap was up in the daytime, the netting was always down. In this way we managed to keep the pests out quite well, but every night before we retired we would take the lamp and go all around the tent and kill off what mosquitoes we could find. It was easy to see them when they would light on that white canvas.

So day after endless day went by with the baby and me cooped up in that tiny tent out of the wind and rain and mosquitoes. The house stood in front of the tent, and now we couldn't even see the creek and the occasional boat passing by. It seemed pretty awful.

When Captain Parker came to stay with us over the July 4th holiday, it was wonderful. He was quite jolly and talked to us about his travels over the world. He was a good carpenter too and helped Ross put a couple of windows into the house and showed him how to make the door frame and several other things that Ross wasn't sure he knew how to do.

Thank goodness the weather behaved while the Captain was there. We laid some boards on the floor joist of the house and spread his bedroll there and hung the mosquito canopy over it, which he had the foresight to bring along. If it had rained, the nights he spent there certainly would have been a mad scramble to get him and his bed into the tent. The holiday ended all too soon, and the good Captain left us to go back to his job, promising, though, to come back and see us again soon. However, he was shifted to another job a few months after his visit, and it was a couple of years before I ever saw him again.

Dad and Ed decided they needed a vacation, so they left intending to be away for a month or 6 weeks visiting Dad's other children who lived up around Orlando and Sanford. Now Ross and I were all by ourselves. It seemed dreadfully quiet with no one at all coming and going. One day while Ross was out to his trotline, a couple of young men started clearing away the underbrush in back of our tent. I went out and asked them what they thought they were doing. They said their Uncle had sent them to clear up a place so he could build a house there.

I told them to spare their efforts and go tell their uncle that he couldn't build there, that we were building a house here and here we were going to stay. I was frightened half to death. In a flash I remembered all the ugly tales that had been told to me in Fort Myers and I wondered what would happen to me now, but I stood my ground and they stood there looking at me for what seemed ages. Then one of them said, "We will go and get our uncle, then we will be back." They turned and made their way back through the underbrush to the north. When I got back into the tent I was shaking like a leaf and I prayed, "Dear God, let Ross be home when they come back." I was in a dreadful state all day. When Ross came in I told him what had taken place and he said, "Good girl, don't let them bluff you." He didn't go back to his trotline any more that day, but they didn't come back for several days. When they did come, there was a Mr. Burnette with them, a man whom I had seen a few times who had a camp on Little Bare Beach. He was the uncle. As usual, Ross was out in the lake and I had to face them alone.

Mr. Burnette asked me why I had stopped the boys from working there. He said he had planned to build there before we ever came to the island. I told him that there was nothing to show that anyone had any such intentions when we settled there, and because we had decided to stay, we were staking a claim and were already building our house, as he could see. He was dreadfully disappointed and said he didn't know just what to do about it, to which I replied there wasn't anything he could do about it. We were here and were going to stay. So they went away and that was the last we heard of that. Mr. Burnette did later settle on the north end of Torry Island and in time we became good friends and neighbors.

July 16, 1912. I'll never forget that date. We were eating our noonday meal when we heard run boat motors chugging away out in the lake. We hastily finished our lunch and, the day being sunny for a change, took the baby and went to the landing to meet the boat. As the boat nosed into the landing, Ross and I stood there aghast. Sitting on the deck were his mother and his brother, George.

Instead of thinking how nice it was to see them, my thoughts were, whatever will we do with them? What about beds? Then too, there was the problem of food. How could we make rations for two stretch enough to feed four?

They got off the boat and when greetings were over, Mother Winne, the baby, and I went to the tent to prepare dinner for the two of them and left Ross and his brother George to attend to unloading the boat. When the box of groceries was brought in I thought, what a pitifully small bundle of groceries for so many people. Fortunately, I had just gotten a barrel of flour the week before and a 30-pound tin of shortening. That at least was a comfort.

When lunch was ready, the men had finished unloading the boat and came in the tent so George and his mother could eat. After they had eaten, Ross said to me, "Now where are we going to put that stuff?"

"What stuff?" I asked. "Why, the stuff that George and Mother brought," he said. "We will have to stack it up in here somewhere, I guess," I replied. "Can't be done," said Ross. "Can't possibly get it all in here." So I went out to have a look.

They had sold our little houseboat that we had left in Ohio for them to live in when we came to Florida, but hadn't sold the furnishings, most of which they stored with friends, but they had brought my sewing machine, a folding bed, and all of my blankets, quilts, and an extra pair of pillows, besides dishes, pots and pans, and various other things. No, we couldn't possibly get them all into the tent, but somehow we had to find a place for the sewing machine and the bedding. The other things that could take the rain were placed in the skeleton of the house on the floor joists to keep them out of the mud.

With the tent full to overflowing, there wasn't room for us to turn around without stepping on one another's feet. When it rained and we all had to be in the tent daytimes, some of us had to sit on the bed cross-legged in order to leave room for the others. There was no floor space for the baby to crawl around in and he became very fretful and cross. At night we put the table outside the tent in order to make a bed on the floor for Ross and George. Mother Winne, young Wilton, and I had the bed.

It nearly always rained in the night, and every morning we had to wash the mud off the table legs before we could bring the table back inside. What a mess! Besides this, with so many going in and out of the tent all the time, it was impossible to keep the mosquitoes out, and my poor baby Wilton was constantly covered with red blotches from mosquito bites.

When the boat left that trip, they said they expected it would be about 10 days before they would be back again because most of the fishermen had gone to the coast for a little vacation. That meant 10 days of short rations. The grocery list I gave the captain certainly looked huge beside the ones I was wont to send, but I knew that there would be very little food left in our camp when they returned. How right I was! The boat didn't return for 2 weeks.

One day when everything went wrong, it rained hard all day and the tent leaked all over; we were having an awful time trying to keep the beds dry when Mother Winne spoke very disgustedly about the weather, the crowded tent, the primitive conditions, and everything else she could think of to complain about. I said, "Now you understand why I wrote that letter asking you not to come until September." Said she, "Yes, I certainly do understand." Then Ross asked, "Well, why did you come now? Gertie certainly told you plain enough." She said, "Well, we had made our plans to come, and we thought if you could stand it, we could." "Then you will just have to stand it," Ross said, "and don't complain. Gertie don't, and you have no one to blame but yourself."

When the boat returned, it brought some of the flooring and the roofing for the house. Ross and George were very busy getting out more trotline and working on the house too. As soon as they had covered half of the roof, they laid a bit of flooring under it, and we moved the stove and table into the house. It was miserable to cook meals while fighting mosquitoes, but it seemed good to have the extra room in the tent.

At the end of 2 weeks when the boat came back again, they brought the last of the lumber for the house, and in a few days we were moved out of the tent. How good it was to have a bit of elbowroom once more!

And then another bombshell! When the boat returned the next trip, who should be on it but Father Winne and Bob Myers, a boyhood pal of Ross. We hadn't gotten the larder sufficiently restocked for the four of us and the baby, and now we had two more to feed and fix beds for. I hardly knew which way to turn.

Despite all that I had told them in letters about how far we were from Fort Myers and how hard it was to have things brought in and how long it took, they still couldn't imagine a place so remote; neither could they believe that there was still a place in the United States that was more than a day's trip for groceries. But they soon learned—and the hard way, at that.

When the boat left on the next trip, Ross told the captain how short of food we were and said he hoped they could manage to come back a bit sooner than they had the last few trips. The captain said he would make a point of getting back in a week or so, which certainly sounded good to us, but it didn't turn out that way.

Since we expected the boat to return in a week or 10 days at most, we portioned out our food to last that long with a little to spare. The 10 days went by, most of the food was gone. We still had flour and shortening in plenty, so our daily diet was fish, bread, and coffee. Then, after a while, just fish and bread. The day we scraped the last bit of flour from the bottom of the barrel, the boat returned. It had been gone more than 3 weeks, and we were all beginning to wonder what would happen to us if it didn't come soon.

Father Winne was the type of person who enjoyed finding fault and blaming others for his discomforts. We were all edgy, the mosquitoes were fierce, and every time the screen door was opened, they swarmed into the house and chewed on everyone. We were all sick of the sight of fish and to have to cook and eat the stuff was an ordeal. The baby was irritable, unaccustomed to so many people around; the mosquitoes were biting day and night and added to this was Father Winne's fault finding. Just listening to him one had the impression that we were to blame for his being there.

When the groceries were brought in from the boat, I couldn't believe my eyes. These certainly were not the groceries I had ordered; besides, the amount was small and we were out of everything.

Then the captain told us the sad story. The fish company we had been doing business with had folded up and gone out of business. Now we were in a mess. We had been sending our fish in to the company, and the company had our grocery orders filled and everything else we needed. All was charged against our account and the balance stayed with the company until Ross would go in and settle it. He had made a settlement of sorts when he ordered the lumber for the house, but he just left the money stand in case we needed more material. Now everything we had was tied up in a defunct fish company.

The groceries that came were through the courtesy of Captain Tom Bass who owned a fish business just a short distance from the one we had been doing business with, and we didn't even know Captain Tom. We were very grateful to him and have since regarded him as one of the grandest men we ever knew.

The boat was returning to Fort Myers at once. The captain and his partner had a considerable amount of their own money tied up in the fish company too, so Ross said he would go back with them and together they would see what the chances were of getting their money. As Ross was leaving, I said, "If you get your money out of those birds, I'd like for you to bring back a couple of chairs and a rocking chair. I'm tired of sitting on hampers and boxes." Dad Winne piped up and said, "You are getting mighty damned high toned. Have to have chairs yet! Can't sit on boxes like the rest of us, eh? The boy will probably have to spend his last cent for 'em." At that, Ross exploded. "What damned business is it of yours? If she wants chairs, I reckon she can have 'em. You don't have to pay for 'em!" And out he stamped.

This news about the fish company was just about the last straw, and we were all nearly at each other's throats, but none of them stopped to think that Ross and I, left to ourselves, could have managed somehow. But Ross was gone, and I had to make the best of it with four disgruntled people endlessly complaining that I was being "stingy" when I tried to stretch the rations. It was a good thing that I was stingy though. The boat was gone for 10 days.

Ross managed to get all of his money out of the company, but the captain and his partner never did get all of theirs. Before they left Fort Myers, they made arrangements with Captain Tom Bass to handle their fish. Ross stocked up on groceries and bought me four dining chairs and a very comfortable sewing rocker, which his dad promptly took over; and when Father Winne was in the house, the chances of anyone else sitting in that rocking chair were very small. He didn't like to sit on boxes or hampers any better than I did.

When they went to Fort Myers, Ross said the canal and Caloosahatchee River were full of water, and 10 days later when they came back, the country was flooded. At La Belle, the whole town was under water; people were going about in boats, the bridge across the river was left open, and the water was just even with the top of the handrail. When they reached the vicinity of old Fort Thompson, Ross looked over the side of the boat and saw they were over a cornfield. While he was looking, they passed over the top of a wire fence. He called to the captain, "Do you know where you are?" "Sure, said the captain, "I'm in the canal." "Like hell you are," said Ross. "You're in somebody's cornfield."

One look over the side was enough for the captain. "Come take the wheel," he said, "and get us back where we belong." Ross climbed on top of the cabin, got his bearings, then came inside and took the wheel. After an hour or so they were back in the canal again.

Ross said he had been greatly worried about us with our few groceries, but they just couldn't hurry things in Fort Myers. He was glad to be home again, and I thought surely everything that could possibly happen to us had happened, and now we ought to be able to settle down to normal living again, if such a thing could be possible with all those extra people in that little house with us. Even had we known they were coming, we couldn't have afforded to build it any larger.

A Visit to the Doctor

Then I got sick. Chills, fever, and aches, one right after the other and with all those people to cook and wash clothes for. I hadn't been feeling well for quite some time, but I blamed the food and living conditions and all the upsetting things that were happening and thought that when we got settled in the house and got our grocery situation straightened out, I'd soon be feeling fit again, but not so.

We did settle down to a hard, monotonous grind. When there was just Ross, Wilton, and me, we had plenty of time for one another with an occasional hour or so up at Dad's camp, but now it was all hard work. No more carefree time.

In the latter part of August, the rains let up and the sun shone once more. This made everyone else feel better, but not me, so Ross thought I should take a trip to Fort Myers and see a doctor. He said he would go in with me because he wanted to see about ordering rope and webbing for nets. Now that we had such a large crew of men around, trotline fishing for such a crowd was out of the question; they all expected Ross to furnish the necessary equipment to fish with, although where the money was to come from to buy it with I couldn't figure.

One day Ross borrowed the little launch belonging to Dad and Ed, and he and his crew made a trip down the Lauderdale Canal to see Captain Parker. When they got back, Ross had a sizable check in his pocket. He had borrowed money from the captain to buy material for nets.

It was about mid-September when we left Wilton with Mother Winne and set out on our trip to Fort Myers. This was the first time I had gone to town since New Year's Day, more than 8 months earlier. It seemed incredible that I had been content to stay isolated on Torry Island.

Even though the thought of seeing civilization was tempting, I wasn't enthusiastic about the trip, because I dreaded the long ride on that same, smelly, uncomfortable boat. It was bad enough on that first trip when I was feeling fit, but now that I was ill most of the time, I had no desire whatsoever to make the trip.

The weather behaved beautifully. The boat was crowded, as it had been on that first trip, and we were able to stir around enough to keep our feet and legs from being numb. When we finally arrived at Fort Myers, I was surprised to discover I wasn't a bit tired.

While Ross went about the business of ordering material for nets, I went to see a doctor, who told me that I merely had a bad case of chills and fever from being down on the swampy lake for so long. He gave me a huge bottle of pills and said that by the time I had taken those I would be fit as a fiddle again.

After this was attended to, we set out to see the town, which really was a disappointment. The town was small, and one could easily see the sights in a day. The only tourist attraction was the home of Thomas Edison, which was open to visitors a few days a week. We never were fortunate enough to tour Edison's home, but we were told that plants from all parts of the world had been imported and planted there. Some flourished, some struggled, and others that couldn't adapt died; however, the whole estate was said to be a place of rare beauty with its exotic plants, shrubs, and trees.

Fort Myers boasted one picture theater, which was open only on Wednesday and Saturday nights. Otherwise, there was no amusement, and after 5 or 6 days, we were glad to be starting back to Torry Island once more.

We left Fort Myers about mid afternoon and ran down to La Belle, arriving there late at night. We tied up to a tree on the bank and tried to sleep until morning. Ross and I had only a blanket spread on the deck, but we managed to catch a little sleep. Just as day was breaking we stepped ashore and went down the bank a little way to wash our faces. We stooped down side by side, and just as I was reaching to cup some water in my hands, Ross pulled me back on my heels. "Look!" he said. There in the water was the most brilliantly colored snake I had ever seen.

"What is it?" we asked the captain. "Good, heavens, man," he said. "That's a coral snake, the most deadly we have in Florida." After they killed the snake, we bathed our faces and were glad to get back on the boat again and resume our trip home.

Life became pretty humdrum after this. With so many men-folk around, the boat was always filled, and there was no room for Wilton and me to go out with Ross to fish his lines; there were no more little jaunts to explore new places. My days were filled with cooking, cleaning, and washing; when everybody was in the house, it was impossible to work without tripping over someone's feet.

I took my medicine faithfully, and in a couple of weeks the chills and fever were gone, but by this time I knew that I was pregnant. I'm afraid I wasn't very happy about it. Fort Myers was 135 miles away; there was no hospital there, and I had no idea where I could go or how I would be cared for. It wasn't pleasant to think about.

Trip to Miami

By the latter part of October the canal was cut through to Fort Lauderdale and boats were allowed to go through, though they could pass the dredge and drill barge only at 6 o'clock in the mornings and evenings, at which time they changed crews. The dredge and barges were pulled to one side of the canal at those hours to allow boats to pass.

The men who owned the run boat had never been to the east coast, so they asked Ross if he would pilot the boat for them and he said he would. On October 17, 1912, Ross took the first boatload of fish from Lake Okeechobee down through the North New River Canal to Fort Lauderdale and on to Miami.

Fort Lauderdale wasn't much of a town in those days either. The town consisted of a grocery store, two department stores, a hardware store, two hotels, and a couple of boarding houses. There were perhaps three blocks of sidewalk and a narrow paved street running through the town connecting with the road from West Palm Beach to Miami.

The fish house was a small one and did not have facilities for handling large amounts of fish, so Ross was forced to go all the way to Miami to dispose of the fish. On the way back from Miami, Ross met Captain Cross, who was taking a load of fish down. He too was strange in those waters, so he asked Ross to go back down with him and pilot his boat and Ross went gladly.

A larger fish house was soon built in Fort Lauderdale, and the long haul to Miami was no longer necessary. It seemed good to know that instead of the 135-mile trek to Fort Myers, we now could go to Fort Lauderdale only 64 miles away.

Luckily for us, the material for Ross's nets came before the fish business was moved from Fort Myers to Fort Lauderdale for as soon as they were certain of continued passage through the canal to Fort Lauderdale, the fish companies began moving their businesses, and by Thanksgiving time the fish business had made Fort Lauderdale a booming town.

By the first of December, the men had the nets all made, and the week before Christmas, Ross, Wilton, and I went to Miami so Ross could show me the town. I had heard so much of Miami that I expected to see something magnificent, but I was terribly disappointed. The streets were white rock and oyster shell, reflecting a blinding sunshine. The outlying streets were like cow trails, narrow and sandy. Its few stores were collected in a couple of blocks of Flagler Street and Miami Avenue, but they were small, nothing like the impressive establishments of today. Occasionally, a store boasted an awning of corrugated iron roofing built out over the sidewalk. While we were in Miami we saw a good baseball game, the only excitement for that trip. If there was a picture theater, we didn't see it; anyway, there were no movies worth seeing in those days.

The one thing that interested me was a small shop built on the edge of the pier, out over the water of Biscayne Bay. On display in this shop were many kinds of shells, all marked as to species and habitat. There were shells from all oceans, but the most beautiful came from the Bahamas. We spent 3 days in Miami, returning home very tired and glad of the relative quiet of our island home.

More to Fishing Than Just Catching Fish

Fishing was very good, and news of it spread like wildfire. Many new people came to the lake to try their luck at fishing, and many of them left in disappointment. They soon learned that there was much more to fishing than just catching the fish. Mending nets and setting them properly and caring for the fish until the boat came for them were most important.

One of the would-be fishermen came from Pompano with his wife and small daughter. He planned to stay with Dad and Ed Simmons and enlarge their business, but a few weeks was enough for them. When they left, they wanted to dispose of their boat, a Jersey sea skiff with an inboard motor. Ross was glad for the chance to buy it. He really needed a motorboat to get around to his nets in a day. Now that we owned a motorboat, I didn't feel quite so panicky and helpless. It meant a chance to get away to town on our own, if necessary, without waiting until the run boat made its regular trips.

Christmas

Christmas came to the island, another strange Christmas. We had neither tree (there would have been no room for it anyway) nor any hustle and bustle of preparing the usual Christmas goodies (no place to put them to keep them from ants and bugs). So on Christmas morning we had a little exchange of gifts and a few toys for the baby.

After breakfast Ross and Bob Kleiser, an acquaintance from West Palm Beach, went out in the lake to shoot some wild duck for dinner, Ross's dad having brought a 12-gauge Winchester pump shotgun to Ross when he came from Ohio. I was determined to have a real Christmas dinner and to make the day as merry and Christmasy as possible, so while Ross and Bob were out getting the ducks, I baked pies and cookies, brought lettuce and radishes from the garden, cut a few green boughs from a rubber tree that grew in the edge of our clearing, dug up a bit of red ribbon from the bottom of the trunk, tied the boughs with a big red bow, placed them in a can of water, and set them on the dish cupboard. This little spot of Christmas green and red gave me quite a boost; it made me feel a little less homesick, and I managed to make a good day of it for everyone. I even popped some popcorn and made a bit of taffy candy, which we all enjoyed.

Baby on the Way

After the holidays we had a rainy spell for a couple of weeks and I began shaking with chills and fever again, so Ross decided that I had better go to Fort Lauderdale and stay until the baby came. I hated the thought of having to stay in town with complete strangers; at such a time a woman wants her own people around her, but there was nothing else we could do, so I was packed off to town to sit and wait.

I hadn't seen a doctor since going to the one in Fort Myers who told me there was nothing wrong with me but chills and fever, so I had no idea how long the waiting might be. Ross had made arrangements for a place for me to stay and be taken care of, but when we got there we were earlier than expected and the lady couldn't take me, so Ross spent a miserable 2 days looking for a place with someone to take care of me and the baby.

He finally found a woman who needed a little extra money and was willing to crowd her family up for a while and make room for me and the baby. This was good news for us, and we were very grateful. I got settled in my room late that afternoon, and early the next morning Ross went back to the lake. I hadn't brought Wilton with me, but Ross promised to come back to town the next trip and bring Wilton to stay with me so I would be less lonely. I at once began counting the days that must go by before the boat's return.

The people with whom I was staying were friendly enough, and I couldn't have asked to be treated more kindly. The family consisted of a husband and wife (who I knew only as Mrs. N.), the wife's two children (4 and 6 years old) by a previous marriage, and the wife's 13-year-old sister, who was sickly most of the time. There were also two men who boarded there, altogether a sizable group of people.

I got the shock of my life that first day when I learned that the entire family dipped snuff, even the two small children. When I was a child at home in Ohio, I had occasionally seen old men who sniffed snuff, but until I came to Florida, I had never known of people taking snuff in their mouths, and to see those two little children dipping snuff like veterans was quite beyond me.

The first few days went by so dreadfully slow. I shook with chills and burned with fever one day and felt fairly well the next. The doctor said I would just have to fight it out because he couldn't give me quinine until after the baby came, so I had that to look forward to also—chills and fever every other day.

Mrs. N received a letter from her brother saying that he and the younger brother were coming to spend a few days with her. After reading the letter she became quite talkative and told me about the family. Waldo, Florida, was their hometown. She and her first husband lived on a ranch a short distance from town. Her parents had died the year before, and these two brothers and the sister all lived with her. Her husband, she said, drank heavily and when he was under the influence of drink was a bully and quite mean. Her eldest brother was 15 years old, and her husband gave him frequent beatings as well as herself. One evening the husband came home in a quarrelsome mood and declared he was going to "whip hell out of the whole outfit." She managed to hide herself in a closet, but her brother decided his brother-in-law had beaten him around for the last time, so he grabbed up the shotgun and killed him. The boy was arrested, spent some time in jail, and was finally released on bond, which was gotten up by various friends and neighbors. After months of waiting, he was finally brought to trial and acquitted.

I certainly didn't relish the idea of living with people who could talk so calmly of a family murder, and it gave me the creeps to think of having a real murderer in the same house with me. When the brothers finally came, it was a pleasant surprise to see two well-mannered, soft-spoken boys, and their few-day stay kept everyone so talkative and jolly that the time passed all too soon.

A few days later I was awakened one night by violent quarreling and the children crying and sobbing, amidst which in a voice of cold fury I heard Mrs. N. say, "I'll kill you for this." I immediately thought of the things she told me concerning the murder of her first husband, and I wondered if she wouldn't do just that. I was too frightened to move, so I clutched my pillow tightly over my ears to shut out their voices and the rest of the night I lay staring into the darkness.

When morning finally came, I reluctantly got out of bed and forced myself to go out to join the family at breakfast, fearful that something dreadful might have happened in the night. When I came to the table, I was surprised to find everyone pleasantly talking. I soon learned that they considered these awful quarrels mere love spats. What a queer way of expressing love for another.

Ross came and brought Wilton while I was still dreadfully upset over that first quarrel. I told him about it and expressed a wish to find some other place for me to stay. He searched the town over, but there was no other place where I could get a room and care, so I had to stay where I was for a time. Each day I wondered if that would be the day or night when one of them would carry out their threat to kill the other, but after a while I realized that their quarreling didn't amount to anything but nasty threats and ugly words, and all was forgotten immediately after.

Wilton was almost 2 years old, just the age to keep a person busy, so that helped me through the week, and on Saturday February 1, 1913, at 9 o'clock in the morning my baby was born, a boy whom we named John Edward, Jack for short. He was a sickly little fellow, pitifully thin with blue skin. The doctor said that now my malaria should leave me and then the baby would get all right too, but he was mistaken. I continued to have a good day, then a bad one. The baby didn't cry much but was fretful and moaned and tossed in his sleep. The doctor didn't do a thing for either of us, just kept saying that it would take a little time and I would have to be patient.

Going Home Again

Time passed slowly and when Jack was 10 days old, Ross came to town to make arrangements to bring the children and me home. During my stay in Fort Lauderdale, the stern wheel steamer Osceola started making regularly scheduled trips between Fort Myers and Fort Lauderdale, one roundtrip a week. Ross managed to get a stateroom on this boat for the children and me while he returned on the fish boat he had come down on.

The boat left Fort Lauderdale on the morning of February 13. Jack was not yet 2 weeks old. Lucky for me, this was my good day, so I managed well though. There were some 16 or 18 passengers on board, one of whom was Thomas E. Will, who was greatly interested in the Everglades and in later years became one of its chief developers. The boat was slow; in fact, it made no better time than the many fish boats that run back and forth from the lake to Fort Lauderdale, but being so much larger was more comfortable to travel on. Late that night we stopped a couple of miles from the lake, tied up to the custard apple trees along the canal bank, and remained until morning.

At daybreak we were under way again, and the call to breakfast came just as we passed out of the canal into the lake. Most of the passengers seemed quite excited about their first glimpse of Lake Okeechobee, but the excitement for me was in the knowledge that I would soon be home. I was anxious to get there as soon as possible because I wanted to be home before the chills and fever started.

The morning was cold with a steady drizzle of rain falling. The wind was from the north and the waves were choppy on the outer edge of South Bay. (The Fort Lauderdale Canal entered the lake at the tip of South Bay.) Some of the passengers were getting seasick and returned to their staterooms.

Jack was still sleeping, but Wilton and I were on deck as soon as we had finished breakfast, eagerly looking toward Torry Island just a short distance away, expecting every minute to see our little launch coming out across the lake to intercept the steamboat and take us home, but no such luck. We went on to the Miami Canal,

where there was a hotel at which several passengers were planning
to stay. This was about 7 or 8 miles from our place on Torry Island.
We had often heard of this hotel but had never been there. The Bolls'
real estate people had built the hotel in 1910 and purchased miles of
Everglades swamp lands in connection with the Everglades drainage
and reclamation project, which was being so strongly promoted at
that time. To build this hotel the material was brought to the lake
from Fort Myers on barges. The site for the building was 3 or 4 feet
under water, so all the work of laying the foundation of wooden
piling was done from boats. The piling was driven with a pile driver
rigged on a barge. After the piling was driven and tied together
and the floor sills in place, the rest of the building was much easier
to manage.

There was a wide verandah all around the house, and on the
east, from the verandah to the canal, a wide boardwalk was built
the same level as the porch floor. On each side of this walk, which
must have been 150 feet long, were built boxes about 3 feet wide
and 18 inches deep. These were filled with muck and planted with
vegetables and flowers so people could see what could be grown in
the muck land if the water were drained from it. These boxes were
new and the vegetable plants were just a few inches high and looked
very attractive, especially with all that water all around under the
walk and the hotel and with the rowboats tied at the door of the
verandah.

The Miami Canal, like the Fort Lauderdale Canal, was being
cut from both ends but wasn't cut through yet; in fact, it was never
entirely finished. There was a Japanese boy working at the hotel who
came out and carried my suitcase and a maid came running out to
get the baby. I was so glad to have this help because I was beginning
to feel shaky and could never have gotten into the hotel by myself.

A Mrs. King and her daughter from Washington, DC, were running the hotel. They made a great fuss over the children and tried to
make me comfortable, but I was shaking with a chill and there was
nothing to be done but let the fever wear itself out. I was trying so
hard to keep people from seeing how sick I was and feeling sorry

for me, and I kept wishing and wishing that Ross would come and take me home.

The morning passed so slowly; the wind out of the north got fresher and colder and still it drizzled. I finally gave up and asked for a bed so I could lie down. I was shaking so I could hardly go up the stairs. All the rooms in the hotel were taken, so Mrs. King took me to her room, tucked me in bed, got the children settled, and then brought me a cup of hot broth, which did a world of good. The chill finally left me and, because the children were both asleep, I too dozed off. I have no idea how long I slept, but I was awakened by the maid who told me that Ross had come for me.

When I bade good-bye to my newfound friends, they made us promise to come back to see them real soon and be sure to bring the children. From that day on we were very good friends and enjoyed many good times together as long as they remained on Lake Okeechobee.

Ross had brought plenty of oilskin coats and canvas, and good thing he did. His mother and brother George had come with him. On the return, George ran the boat, Ross and his mother held the children, and it was all I could do to hold myself together. The lake was so very rough, and it was still rainy. We all would have been drenched in that boat if we hadn't had those oilskins.

I stayed in bed for several days getting over that trip, but I couldn't get rid of the malaria, so I began to take the quinine. The baby didn't improve and was hungry all the time, so I started giving him canned cream. There was no place to get bottles, so I fed him with a spoon. When we did get a bottle for him, he wouldn't have it, so I kept on feeding him with a spoon, and by the time he was 6 weeks old, he was drinking from a glass. He still didn't gain any weight, and, on top of all this, I discovered that his spine was crooked. Every day I massaged his back with castor oil, and I made several heavy binders lined with flannel and kept these pinned tightly around him. In a month, I could tell that his back was straightening.

The weather continued cold and rainy. On my good days, I worked in my garden as much as possible, though with two babies

to care for and all those men to feed, I didn't have much time for anything else, but I managed and soon had my garden back in order.

One cold, rainy day about the middle of March, the surveyors
came. We could hardly believe it. We had sent our petition to Washington less than a year before, but the surveyors were here already.
Naturally, we were elated. We loaned them our small boats, which
made it much easier for them to get their equipment around. They
were very grateful.

There were three creeks on Torry Island and one on Kreamer,
but the creek in front of our house was the only one that was given
a name. They called it Winne Creek, and the indentation in the
shoreline north of the creek they called Winne Cove. Soon after
the surveyors had finished their work on the islands, Mr. Waggoner
got busy with another petition to the Department of the Interior
requesting that the islands in Lake Okeechobee, namely, Torry, Little
Kreamer, and Ritta, be declared homestead land.

Fishing had been extra good that spring and Ross had to turn
thousands of pounds of fish back into the lake because he had no
way to get them to market. The men who owned the freight boats all
had nets of their own and the boats were mostly loaded with their
fish, so Ross decided it was time to buy a boat and haul his own fish.
He went to Fort Lauderdale and spent a week looking around. He
finally found a boat to his liking, but it couldn't be made ready for
the rest of the spring fishing, so he had to content himself to wait
for fall for it.

And now, we got new neighbors. A Scotsman, Mr. McLaughlin,
and his wife set up a camp on the south end of Torry Island, and
a man from LaBelle came to fish with Dad and Ed Simmons and
brought his wife and 15-year-old daughter with him. Just knowing
there were other women on the island besides my mother-in-law and
me made life seem more bearable and much less lonely.

6

Home Again

Back to Ohio

The malaria stayed with me. When June came and George was getting ready to go back to Ohio, Ross said I had better take the children and go too. Perhaps the change of climate would do something to rid me of those chills and fever every other day. Ross would come a month or so later and stay the rest of the summer, then we could come back to Florida together in the fall.

So, off we went. We left Fort Lauderdale on the night of June 4th. Arriving in Jacksonville the next morning, the weather was so dreadfully cold and no heat in the station, we all suffered terribly. When we boarded the train after a four-hour wait, everyone was blue with cold and all were sneezing and sniffling dreadfully. My poor baby, who was always so blue looking anyway, turned purple from the cold. At that time of year, no one had carried enough warm clothing for such a sneak cold spell as that. We were all glad to be in a steam-heated train. It seemed hours before we were warm again.

Somewhere in Tennessee we had a wait of several hours. There had been a train wreck ahead of us, and we had to wait until the tracks were cleared before we could go on. We hadn't sent any word to my mother and father that I was coming home, so my arrival was a big surprise. I was truly glad to be home once more and glad too that the long train trip was over.

The malaria must have been frozen out of me in Jacksonville because my chills and fever didn't come back any more, and in a week or so, I was feeling like my old self again. It was wonderful to be home, to be in a real honest-to-goodness house again instead of a shack, and to have all my old friends dropping in to see me. It was just like old times and made me realize how much I had missed all of this neighborliness and companionship.

Ross came the first week in July, and we had a wonderful summer visiting here and there, going to dances, parties, picnics, and helping with the harvest by gathering fruit and canning. When duck hunting season came in, Ross had several wonderful days out in the old familiar marshes hunting and shooting wild ducks. Then, all too soon, it was time to return to Florida.

No one but me ever knew how much I dreaded returning to Florida. Going back to that little shack home on Torry Island in the heart of the swampy Everglades with the bugs, mosquitoes, lizards, crawling snakes, and all sorts of wild animals, squawking birds, and loneliness—most of all, the loneliness.

Back to Florida

Life goes on somehow despite one's feelings, so early in October we bade farewell to family and friends and once again wended the tortuous route back to Florida, which seemed even worse than the trip before. Arriving in Fort Lauderdale, we were lucky to find a boat leaving the next day for Lake Okeechobee, and, tired as we were, we were glad to be getting the trip over with and once more settling down to the business of making a living and being at home again.

The surprises that awaited us were unbelievable! A place called Okeelanta about 3 miles from the lake on the Lauderdale Canal had sprung up while we were away. The Tilton Hotel was on one side of the canal and a store and a post office, mind you, on the other side of the store. During the summer the mail route was shifted and now came by way of Fort Lauderdale instead of Fort Myers. The store and post office were owned and operated by a Mr. Baker and his wife. A few houses were under construction. How exciting to have a store and post office so near! The store carried groceries, farmer's boots and shoes, men's dungarees and work shirts, gasoline, small supplies for boats, hardware, cultivators, harnesses, and other items. It also carried samples of materials from a large store in Fort Lauderdale from which the ladies could select materials for clothing. Mr. Baker would send the order in on the first boat going down and the material would be brought out on the next trip. It was very convenient for women who didn't go to Fort Lauderdale more often than once a year or perhaps not that often. Sears Roebuck and Co. also did a lot of business in those days on Lake Okeechobee, especially when parcel post came in around that time.

There was no settlement at Ritta, but the water in the Glades and the lake had gone down and the mainland was now above water. A few people were settling around the south end of the lake with a few patches of ground being cleared and planted, but transportation was still a problem and no boats for carrying vegetables had as yet come to the lake. What garden plots there were were small and mostly experimental. Fishing was still the means of making a living.

Our little house on Torry Island was quite crowded. Mother and Father Winne had stayed there through the summer. When Ross left to come to Ohio to join me, a young man called Red came to stay with the old folks and to fish a few trotlines. Now, besides him, there were Ross's brother George and two men from Ohio. With Ross, the two children, and me, there were 10 people in that tiny shack. It was impossible to move around without having to step over the feet of someone sprawled on the floor. Ten people crammed into a room 14 by 16 feet is just too damn many! Nerves get edgy mighty easy, especially if the weather is bad and everyone has to be inside. If it hadn't been for the attic room overhead, we could never have kept them at all.

In a few weeks, Ross got word that his boat was ready, so he went down to Fort Lauderdale to bring it home and also to get material for more nets, trotlines, and lumber for more boats. Ross bore all of this expense, and for what? Just because a bunch of people descended on us uninvited and expected Ross to furnish jobs and a place to live for them! All of the extra work and inconvenience piled on me was never taken into consideration; it was just expected of me as a matter of course.

Ross had expected to be away only a couple of days, but it was many weeks before he returned. The motor in the boat gave him a lot of trouble and had to be completely overhauled. The thing never did work right, and when the season was well under way, it had to be replaced with a new one. The boat was a large one compared with others on the lake. It was 45 feet long with a 14-foot beam. The ice-box was huge and carried a large amount of fish. When Ross finally got the boat home, I looked it over and thought, "Now I will be able to make an occasional trip to the coast with Ross and won't be so tied down with that crowd of people yakking all the time," but I was disappointed in this too. Ross chose to let one of the men and his dad run the boat, and he stayed with the crew. In all the time we operated that boat, I made just one trip to the coast on it and one trip to Ritta.

Editor's Note

Gertie and Ross stayed in the Florida Everglades and expanded their family. They lived in the tent for 6 months after arriving on Torry Island. It took 3 months to bring the building materials from Fort Myers to the island to build a small 14 x 16-foot house.

After Wilton and Jack, Gertie gave birth to Herman (Smiddy), Mary, Dot, and Ross Jr. Their small home on Torry Island was completed later in 1912. It had two rooms downstairs and two rooms upstairs with 2 covered porches, one on the front and one on the back of the house. Needless to say, this small house was very crowded with 5 adults and 2 young children in it. Ross continued to fish commercially and Gertie continued to manage home, children, and an ever-expanding vegetable garden. Ross's father returned to Ohio later that year and was followed soon after by Ross's mother and brother. Ross's father died in 1920. Ross brought his mother back to Florida soon after, and she lived with Ross and Gertie until her death in 1926.

The population in South Florida boomed with the completion of the Florida East Coast Railroad. The City of West Palm Beach developed rapidly as well. Many of the newly settled residents of South Florida were very interested in the fishing on Lake Okeechobee. Ross expanded his business from commercial fishing to include guiding fishing parties on the lake. Very quickly, those sportsmen became enthralled with the plentiful duck hunting on the lake as well.

Guiding hunting and fishing parties grew, and Ross and Gertie needed a place to house their guests, who often stayed for several days to hunt and fish. Plans were drawn up for a large two-story lodge to be built on the bank of Winne Creek. Many prominent sportsmen sought out the opportunity to hunt and fish with Ross.

The government survey of the islands was completed in the spring of 1913 and island residents immediately petitioned Washington, D.C. to declare the islands homestead land. More settlers began arriving and by late 1914, and all the land on Torry Island and the other islands was completely staked out for homesteading. Vegetable farming became a profitable enterprise for all. The people in the cities needed fresh foods and the Glades area could supply two to three crops each year. Also in 1914, Fletcher Freeman ran the first freight boat to haul fresh vegetables from the islands to the east coast.

The government declared the islands homestead land in 1916 and residents rushed to file their claims. The Winne family filed their claim. The Island Land Board at once contested the homestead claim, but the family won. The Board then contested the right of the government to give land patents to the homesteaders. The government won. Homestead deeds were approved.

The election year of 1916 showed the Ritta Island precinct to be the largest in Palm Beach County.

The islands were now populated and the stark isolation endured by Gertie in her earliest days on the island was gone. A midwife delivered her third child, Herman, on Torry Island. The baby weighed in at 13 pounds. The midwife commented to Gertie, "Mrs. Gertrude, I swear, that big baby slipped out and I done 'swallered' my snuff!" Medical doctors delivered the remaining three Winne children.

Ross Winne began advocating the construction of a road between West Palm Beach on the east coast and Lake Okeechobee in 1919 To reach West Palm Beach, one first had to travel by boat to Fort Lauderdale, then up the coast to West Palm Beach. This trip took 4 days, at best. The County Commission was not favorable at first but finally agreed to allocate $32,000 toward building the road. The road grade was built in 1927/28, providing direct access from Lake Okeechobee to West Palm Beach, a distance of about 40 miles.

Ross decided it was definitely time to build a larger home for his family and for his hunting and fishing patrons. Gertrude's father, Julius Petersen, came to the island in 1923 to construct the new home, generally referred to as "The Lodge." The house was a large 3-story building. Living quarters were on the first two floor and the third floor was like a large open barracks and contained cots to house the hunting and fishing parties who came and often stayed for several days to a week or more. The house was completed in 1924.

Before 1928, the island was entirely cut off from the mainland, boats being the only means of transport; but in the spring of 1928, a muck road grade was dredged up and bridges built connecting the islands of Torry, Kreamer, and Little Kreamer with the mainland. The only roads out of Belle Glade at that time were the one to West Palm Beach and one north to Canal Point, also connecting with West Palm Beach. People weren't very hurricane conscious in those days. They had no idea what to expect or how dangerous wind and water could be.

– Patricia Winne Adams

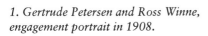

1. Gertrude Petersen and Ross Winne, engagement portrait in 1908.

2. Gertrude and Ross Winne with Wilton (standing) and John Edward.

3. Gertrude Winne, sons WIlton (called Bill), John Edward (Jack), and Herman (Smiddy).

4. Winne children Mary, Herman, and Dorothea. Mary and Dorothea holding celluloid windmills and Herman has a little airplane that he made.

5. *Ross and Gertrude Winne by the small house on Torry Island.*

6. *Busy day on Lake Okeechobee. Duck hunters after a trip guided by Ross Winne. Winne Creek in background.*

7. *Torry Island barn.*

8. *Winne home on Torry Island, Lake Okeechobee. Taken in 1924 shortly after the house was built. This house was commonly called "The Lodge" because the top floor accommodated guests who booked guided hunting and fishing parties with Ross Winne. The top floor was a large, open room with cots.*

Part II

1928 and 1949 Hurricanes in the Florida Everglades

1

Hurricane of 1928

*I*n the week preceding the storm, the Palm Beach papers had carried daily advisories. The forward movement of the storm was only about 7 miles per hour so much had been written about its area, but little about its wind velocity.

On Saturday, September 17, 1928, the West Palm Beach papers said that the hurricane was due to strike Florida sometime Sunday afternoon. In the sky all that day, the cirrus clouds were crisscrossing and the wind held steadily north-northeast.

On Sunday morning the sky was overcast, the rain came in quick, short spurts, and the wind still held NNE. While I was busy with baking and cooking the Sunday dinner, Ross and the three boys went to Belle Glade to get the papers and the latest report on the storm from the Miami Weather Bureau.

Dinner was ready when they returned, so while we ate, we discussed the storm. The report from the Weather Bureau at 10:00 a.m. had indicated that the storm had passed by and there was no danger.

"I don't believe that," said Ross. "If the storm had passed, the wind would have shifted; and it hasn't shifted at all since yesterday."

So we watched the wind and the water, trying to decide whether to leave the island or stay out the storm at home. Our house stood on the north bank of Winne Creek, a scant quarter-mile from the edge of Lake Okeechobee. Ross put a gauge in the edge of the creek, a stick notched in inches. When the water in the creek rose 6 inches in 15 minutes, Ross said, "It's time to go."

While I threw a change of clothing for the girls and myself into a small suitcase, Ross and the boys went out to moor the boats and to try to persuade the people across the creek to come along to the mainland as we were doing. But they said they weren't afraid and would stay on, if we would let them stay in our house, which was three stories high. We told them that they were welcome, but we wished that they would change their minds and come with us.

When they declined, Ross and the boys got a coil of rope from the attic. Making one end of it fast to our front porch, they stretched the rope across the creek, fastening the other end to our neighbor's house so if the wind was too strong for them to row the boat across the creek, they could pull across by the rope. We gave them the key to our house and told them good-bye, still entreating them to come along, but they could not be persuaded.

While doing my baking that morning, I had baked a large gingerbread, and as we were ready to leave, the children begged me to bring it with us. "No," I said, "We'll leave it here and have it when we come home." Wrapping it carefully in wax paper, I packed it in a metal breadbox and set it on top of the kitchen cabinet, thinking to keep it dry even though the lake did rise. The fates must have been laughing, even then.

That morning when Ross and the boys had gone to Belle Glade, they had driven the car and a light pick-up truck. Leaving the car on the mainland, they had come back by truck, parking it on the road about a quarter of a mile from the house. When we were finally ready to leave, we started walking out to the road. The water was rising so rapidly that we had to take off our shoes and wade the last part of the way.

As we drove past the houses of other neighbors, we called to them that we were leaving and urged them to come too. Only one family took our advice and came over to the mainland when we did.

When we got to Belle Glade, it was a few minutes after 3 o'clock. We stopped for gas at the town's one filling station, where a number of men had gathered. One man had just driven out from West Palm Beach. He said that the storm was severe when he left. Windows were blowing out and trees blowing down. Everyone begged us not to go there, but thinking of the water behind us and the wind before us, we decided to go meet the wind.

At that time, there was only a low muck dike around the southern end of Lake Okeechobee, and we felt sure that with wind and water against it, it would not hold. Ross tried to persuade the people that they were more in danger from the lake than from the wind, but they were of different opinions.

At last we started for West Palm Beach. The rain still came in squally patches, and the wind was increasing steadily, but we made good time until we headed eastward from the Twenty-Mile-Bend. Then we were obliged to make the car crawl down the road sideways like a crab. The wind had shifted to the north and struck the car broadside, so to proceed at all, Ross had to steer quartering into the wind.

Finally, we came to a stretch of road where a heavy growth of timber and underbrush on the north side afforded some protection, and for a few minutes we could drive straight ahead. But when we emerged from this sheltered spot, the wind was whooping furiously, and once more we were going down the road sideways.

By the time we reached Military Trail on the outskirts of West Palm Beach, the rain was lashing the earth in wind-driven sheets; and when we headed north on the trail, the wind and rain struck us dead on. We had gone no more than 500 feet when the motor drowned out, and the car came to a sudden stop.

We sat for a few minutes in dreadful silence. Finally, Ross said he had better get out and push the car around, back to the wind, and get the wheels off the hard surface and into the sand. Otherwise, the wind would easily blow us backward into the Palm Beach Canal He got out of the car, opening the door as carefully as possible, but nevertheless, the wind caught it, jerked it right from his hands, and swung it open so forcibly as to spring the hinges. The sprung hinges and the wind together gave him a tussle to close the door again, but at last he managed it; then he set to work turning the car around and pushing it into the sand at the roadside. For added safety, he found two huge rocks and placed them in front of the back wheels for chocks.

By that time, he was afraid to try to get back into the car again for fear of wrecking the other door, so he squatted down in front, as much in the lee as possible, and we all just waited. All this time the wind was blowing terrifically. The tall pine trees in the fields beside the road were bending until their tops swept the ground. The air was filled with small flying objects, and the sheeted rain made a mist through which it was hard to see. The wind finally shifted enough so that Ross could get back into the car, and we were all thankful to have him inside, out of the lashing wind, rain, and cutting sand. He came back just before all hell began breaking loose.

To the east of the road a short distance away were the buildings of a small dairy and adjoining it were the various small shelters of the Palm Beach Country Club. These were being tossed and broken to bits; the debris filled the air all around us. I felt sure some of the wreckage would soon be upon us, so I made the children fit the suitcase into the rear window of the car and hold it there with their heads.

About that time, the whole dairy began falling before the wind. At one end of the barn was a high tower supporting a water storage tank. The tower collapsed and the tank fell, bursting when it hit the ground. The wind picked it up, bowled it along toward us, and gently curled it around the back of the car.

Soon after this, the buildings started tearing apart, and as we watched, fascinated and frightened, the roof of the barn came off in one piece and was blown straight at us. We all knew that the end had come, but just as it was but a few feet away, it parted in two, half of it passing us on either side, so close that we could have reached out and touched it, but not a splinter hit the car.

From then on, the wreckage of buildings, broken timbers, and implements flew around us thick and terrifyingly fast. Even the pitchforks went sailing through the air. During all this, the car surged and swayed like a mad ship but did not break loose from its mire of sand. Then when we were sure the wind would never stop, the lull came.

One moment the storm was on in all its fury; the next, all was calm and deathly still. Even the rain lessened and fell quietly as in the twilight of a spring day. We couldn't believe it. It was too much for our numbed senses to grasp. Our youngest son, aged 12, said, "It's over. Only my prayers saved us, Mama."

Somehow that brought us to our senses. Because it was not over, as we well knew. Ross and the boys got stiffly out of the car to see what they could do about starting it again. Outside, they fairly gasped in surprise. Behind the car several heavy timbers had been driven into the asphalt pavement, some of them within 3 feet of the car; and piled around us was all sorts of wreckage. The car itself had been scoured clean of paint by the flying sand.

Ross and the boys cleared away the wreckage and debris, then they all pushed until they got the car back onto the pavement and headed for town again. The wind had rocked the car back and forth, working the wheels into the sand the depth of the tires.

When they raised the hood, water was standing in every depression in the motor and the wires were drenched. I took several handkerchiefs out of the suitcase and gave them to Ross, and he managed to dry the wires and the motor with these. Then they pushed the car down the road until finally it started.

By this time, darkness was falling. Just as our car started, another car came out of a side road headed for town, too, with a man and his wife inside. They told us their house had been demolished and they were on their way to find shelter in West Palm Beach. The two cars kept together, and good thing we did. Trees, telephone and power lines, and all sorts of wreckage were strewn over the roads. Sometimes it took all hands to clear a path.

By the time we reached the Dixie Highway (US Highway 1), the lull was over and the second part of the hurricane came on us, blowing from the opposite direction of the first half. In the glare of the headlights, we saw buildings completely demolished, others unroofed, windows blown out, and automobiles overturned. A few cars had been blown over the curb into dooryards and turned over. The streets were a mess of broken glass and rubble.

When we had gone a few blocks north on Dixie, a man standing in the lee of a building motioned us on with a flashlight. At Fern Street we were stopped by a policeman and told to go to the Bell Telephone Building, which is on Fern Street between Dixie and South Olive. When we stopped in front of the Telephone Building, a policeman came and opened the door to help us out. Then he said to Ross, "Let me have your keys. We need this car for relief work. There are people in the south end of town who are injured and need help. The only other two cars in town that will run are out on calls." Ross gave him the keys, told him of the broken door, said, "Good luck," and then we all got inside out of the storm.

Ross was a deputy sheriff at that time, and he was soon put to work on special police duty. People were streaming into the building. Some were injured; these were taken to another room made into a first aid center where they received medical attention. Others were screaming with hysteria and fright; these too were given attention. In the first aid room, supplies were running low and they called for volunteers to go to the American Legion Home on the next street for some first aid kits. Ross and another man, whose name he never learned, volunteered to go.

To reach the Legion Home, they had to go east half a block to Olive Avenue, north a block, then east again for half a block. They traversed the half block safely until they reached the corner at Olive Avenue. The water from Lake Worth was 6 inches deep on Olive Avenue, and when they hit that water, footing was uncertain. The wind picked Ross up and raced him across Olive Avenue on tiptoe; it caught the other man and sent him rolling over and over, straight toward the lake.

On the east side of Olive Avenue was a light standard, and as Ross raced along, he flung out his left arm and caught the light standard in the crook of his elbow. Just at that moment, his partner was rolling past. Ross made a lucky grab with his right hand and snatched his jacket. The wind caught the two of them and swung them around the lamppost like whirling dervishes. The weight and fury of it almost wrenched Ross's arm from its socket; all the skin was wrung away. They were flung with such force that, had they fallen, their skulls would have been crushed.

They were just a few steps away from the entrance to the Harvey building, and as soon as they could stand, they made their way to it and stood inside out of the storm to catch their breath. They had been there only a few minutes when a dreadful rending crash came down through the center of the building.

The man cried out, terrified, "I'm getting out!"

"Not me", said Ross. "I'm staying right here."

"But we'll be buried alive!"

Ross shouted back, "Our chances are better here. Out there, we might be blown into the lake and drowned. And besides, there's more wreckage flying around out there."

The next day Ross learned that the chimney, which was 14 stories tall, was what had come crashing down through the building. When the wind died down a bit, Ross and his companion ventured out again. This time they reached the Legion Home, secured the kits, and returned without further incident.

The Bell Telephone Building is one of the most strongly constructed in the town with copper weather stripping around windows and doors. Despite this, the rain was driven in, and water sprawled in puddles on the floor.

About 3 o'clock in the morning the storm had died down enough so we could all breathe again. Everyone who could laid down on the wet floor and tried to rest. Dawn came at last. The wind was still strong and the rain continued steadily. Some friends of ours who lived nearby invited us home with them. "Provided," they said "That there is a home." So we straggled out into the street to wha seemed like a different town. Wreckage everywhere, awnings torn to shreds, frames bent and broken like skeletons, windows smashed, and curtains whipped to strings. A concrete bakery had exploded, and its rubble filled the street.

Our friend's house was a mess. The roofing was gone, many of the windows broken, and everything inside was soaked. There was no gas for cooking, but we rescued two small oil heaters, fortunately almost full of oil, and, with rainwater caught in pails under the eaves, set on a pot of coffee and some oatmeal. The children found some washtubs in the alley. These they set under the eaves to catch water for use in the bathroom.

Meantime, Ross was trying to get the car started. It had been in use until 3 o'clock in the morning before it was finally parked and the keys returned to Ross, but just these few hours later, it wouldn't even cough. There were no garages open and no place to go for help.

Ross wanted desperately to get the car running so he could try to get back to the lake again. After breakfast, he went to the sheriff's office and had a talk with Sheriff Bob Baker. Ross told Bob that he was sure the area around the south of Lake Okeechobee was in dire need of help and asked him to get rescue trucks rolling just as soon as possible.

Bob then asked Ross what would be needed. "You know more about that country than anyone else," he said, "So tell us what we should do and we will do it." Ross told him that first they would need axes, shovels, hammers, and saws—tools for clearing the road. Then they would need food and water and, after that, boats and more boats. Within the hour trucks with crews for clearing the roads were rolling toward the lake country. Ross told Bob that he was having trouble with his car, but as soon as he could get it in order, he was heading out to the lake too. Bob said, "Well, get out there as soon as you can and take charge of things."

It was nighttime before the car was running, so Ross decided to wait until morning before starting out. The weather was still vile— windy with the rain pelting dismally. During the day I had managed to find a place at the Lorain Hotel where we could all sleep dry, although crowded. The children were given pallets on the floor.

Ross was to do guard duty till 2:00 a.m. This would give him time for a bit of sleep before setting out for Belle Glade the next morning. It seemed dreadful to have to wait so long before he could get back there. Knowing the country as we did, we feared the worst. Ross's patrol was in the vicinity of the First Methodist Church of West Palm Beach, which had been turned in to a refugee center.

The first truck to return from the Glades came in about 10 o'clock that night loaded with men, women, and children. Ross said if he lived to be a hundred, he would never forget the look on those people's faces—utter hopelessness and despair; some of the people looked so blank and bewildered they had to be led by the hand. An elderly man whom we had known for years didn't recognize Ross and had to be told who he was. These were our neighbors and friends.

Some of the younger people who were more collected told Ross that Sunday night had been a night of horror. By the time darkness fell, buildings had begun to blow away and water was a foot deep all over town. A number of people had taken refuge in one of the big hotels. Soon after dark, the building began to go, and at the same time, the levee must have given way. They started out to look for another shelter, through wind, water, and darkness. Some lost their footing. A little girl of 4 years was blown from her father's arms. Miraculously, he managed to find her again. They finally reached another building, which stayed in one piece during the storm, although the water rose to the second floor. Another house with 20 people in it had drifted around, finally crossed the canal and sank; another house sank with one end in the canal and the other on the bank. Everyone was drowned.

Only three buildings in the town remained on their foundations the others were demolished or blown helter-skelter all over the country. The only food the people who had remained on the island had had was some canned goods they managed to dig out of the wreckage of grocery stores. They had eaten it cold. It had rained all day so the problem of drinking water was solved by salvaging washtubs from the hardware store and catching rainwater in them. During the morning an old milk cow had wandered into town from somewhere, and someone milked her, and the milk was given to the children.

After this sort of breakfast, a consultation was held, and it was decided that all who wanted to go would start out walking toward West Palm Beach because they felt sure help would be coming from there and would meet them somewhere on the road. They scrambled over wreckage, waded through water, and bogged through mud and hyacinths as far as Six Mile Bridge, where the truck from West Palm Beach met them and brought them into town. It must have been a dreadful trek—the stronger helping the weaker, the little children crying, and everyone tired, hungry, and thirsty, full of the knowledge of the hovering death and destruction behind them, unable to comprehend the miracle of their own escape.

This was the story Ross brought to me when he came off duty at 2 o'clock. We were too utterly heartsick to think of sleep, so we talked on until it was time to be up and getting him and the two oldest boys started on their way to the Glades.

I was coming down with an awful cold. By the time Ross and the boys were ready to leave, my throat felt as though it was closing up, and by noon I couldn't speak a word. I was really quite ill and should have been in bed, but who could lie abed with the thought of other people's greater miseries pressing in on one? That night the two boys came back to West Palm Beach, but Ross didn't come back for 5 days; then he came only for a bath, a change of clothes, and a night's rest.

The task of getting things organized and keeping them moving was enormous. When Ross arrived in Belle Glade Tuesday morning, boats were being unloaded from trucks that had come in during the night. Some were equipped with outboard motors, others only with oars. After seeing the boats under way, starting on their gruesome missions, Ross got into the boat he had reserved for himself. Just as he was shoving off, the local druggist called to him and asked to go with him. The druggist said afterward that he couldn't let Ross go out to the islands by himself because of what he knew they would find when they got there.

Death. Death and destruction were everywhere. Some 2,000 or 3,000 people lay dead, scattered over the countryside, and everything was under water except the islands, although during the storm the water must have covered them 10 or 12 feet deep. On the islands everything was swept clean except for two houses that had been built on pilings to provide for packinghouse and truck space underneath. Our own house was entirely washed away; all that remained were the broken foundations of reinforced concrete, the cement walks all broken and twisted, the bricks from the chimney all scattered about, and a 500-pound fireproof safe had washed entirely outside the foundations. They found it mired down 50 or 75 feet away.

Later Ross learned what had happened to the neighbors who had planned to stay in our house. They had finally been persuaded to leave by two young men calling that day on the two daughters, but they left too late and could not get to the mainland; so with several others, they decided to stop at a new, well-built packinghouse and tool shed, which was about half a mile from the dike. There were 22 people in that building, and only 11 survived.

Lake Okeechobee is a shallow lake, and strong wind sweeps the water before it. Thus, in a hurricane, the water is forced to terrific heights. Inside the packinghouse the water rose steadily. The people climbed first on top of the trucks and tractors, then onto the ceiling joists. When they realized the building could not stand, they forced a hole through the galvanized iron roof, and some of them managed to crawl through. But the water rose so swiftly that the others could not get out. Trapped, they went down with the building. Those who did get out were either blown or washed from the roof as the building went down. Some were drowned at once, some washed away and drifted over the mainland. The survivors were scattered miles apart. One was picked up on Tuesday morning more than 6 miles away. She was still living but unable to walk. So it was everywhere—the living and the dead.

When the boats returned that first night, and each night thereafter for 5 days, they were loaded with the dead. All day Ross went about the task of helping to bring in the dead, and after dark he would go down the rows of coffins and officially identify each one. It was truly a gruesome thing to be called on to do, but it had to be done, and he was the one to have to do it because he knew nearly everyone in the country. When he put the identifications on our neighbor man from across the creek, our nearest and dearest friend who had died helping others to escape from the doomed packing house, it was almost too much for Ross, and he gave way to his feelings, much to the concern of all there who knew him. They tried to persuade him to go in to West Palm Beach that night, but he said, "No, after tomorrow identification will be impossible, so I'll wait until then."

It is hard to imagine what those rescue parties went through at that time. There was no water fit for use except what was hauled out from West Palm Beach. After handling the dead all day, they would all go to a tub of disinfectant and wash their hands in that, then to another tub of medicated water to rinse; then all would go into the improvised mess hall and try to eat, the smell of disinfectant still on their hands and the smell of death in their nostrils. Most of them were unable to eat. Ross lost 14 pounds the first week.

The first 3 days following the storm, the weather had been quite cool; but after that, it was sultry. By the fifth day of rescue work, it was almost unbearable. Tons of fish, rabbits, and other wildlife had been drowned too, and the stench of all this mixed with the odor of decaying bodies was almost more than a man could stand. It was imperative that every few days these workers spend a day or so in West Palm Beach away from the death and decay.

When Ross came in on that fifth day, his first thought was for a hot bath. He bathed, shaved, and started to dress, but changed his mind and got back into the tub again. He said he could still smell that odor on him. When Ross came in to his meals, he could scarcely eat. He would get his hands nearly to his face, then shudder and put them down again, until finally, he forced himself to eat.

At Woodlawn Cemetery in West Palm Beach, steam shovels dug long trenches and the rough-hewn coffins, placed side by side in the common grave, were quickly covered again. A few people complained to the authorities about the smell from the cemetery and wanted them to stop bringing in the dead for burial. I wonder what they would have done if it had been their dead.

When Ross returned to the Glades on the sixth day, further identification was out of the question. The bodies were too badly decomposed to be moved, so the workers carried quick lime with them. When they found a body, they covered it with lime and marked the place so that after the water went down they could come back and bury the remains.

In the cemetery in West Palm Beach, a monument was erected to all those from the Glades who had been drowned in the storm, and on a Sunday, 4 weeks after the hurricane, funeral services were held and the monument unveiled. The cemetery was crowded with people coming all the way from Homestead and Fort Pierce. Throughout the services, all stood with bowed heads and tear-strewed faces. This hurricane tragedy of the Everglades was beyond anyone's imagination.

A week later, 5 weeks after the storm, I made my first trip back to Belle Glade. From what Ross had told me, I felt that I was prepared for what I would see, but somehow it really didn't register until I actually saw the country for myself. I could scarcely believe my eyes. The buildings floated away off from where they belonged; the wreckage of others, the orderly little town, was just a scrambled heap. The railroad tracks had washed away and one part was more than a mile from the roadbed. The ties were still fast to the rails and were standing on end, looking like a giant picket fence.

The road from Belle Glade north to Pahokee was badly washed away, and for most of the way, there was room for only one car to travel, with an occasional place wide enough for passing. From Pahokee north, there was plenty of wind damage, but no water damage until one got as far north as Upthegrove Beach, where the last half of the storm drove the lake over the beach. This part of the country wasn't as thickly populated as the south end of the lake, so the death toll hadn't been nearly so great.

In Canal Point we were fortunate enough to rent a small house that had been blown off the foundations and could be restored without too much trouble. By the middle of the week, Ross, the boys, and I had raised the house back on the foundation, had got together a bit of furniture, and moved in.

I hardly knew if I was glad to be settled back in the Lake Country again or not. Sometimes the cold chills would creep over me, and I had the feeling of living in a graveyard. It took us several years to push the awfulness of what had happened into the back of our minds. Ross' nerves were near the breaking point, and at just the mention of the storm and the few awful weeks that followed, he could scarcely keep from bursting into tears.

I did not see Torry Island again till some time in February 1929. The bridges were still out, so we had to make the trip by boat. When I stepped out of the boat onto what had been our front yard, the emptiest feeling I ever felt came over me. The lawn was so beautiful and green; there were two trees still standing, and that was all, except for the broken foundation of our home and the cracked and broken sidewalks. The full realization of our loss was real to me then. I looked out across our empty farm and saw my youth slipping away from me.

I had been not yet 20 when we came to Torry Island, and for 16 years I had put my youth, my heart, and my dreams into building a home for us all and a future for our children; now it was all gone, and many of our dear friends were dead. Nothing was left but the bare land, and here we were, two middle-aged people with five children to care for. I couldn't imagine how we could ever acquire the courage to start all over again. But courage is restored to one somehow, and each day we managed to pick up a few of the loose ends of our existence and, in time, were again working and planning for the future, along with the other survivors.

Just how well we worked and planned was fully demonstrated to us and to the nation during the recent war (World War II), when

Belle Glade received the Army Award for Outstanding Agricultural Activities and Production, and the Belle Glade section of the Everglades was named the nation's winter vegetable basket.

Gertie had probably thought that she had survived her last hurricane, but in 1949 her family was to be tested again by the weather. The following is a letter she wrote to her daughter Mary, who lived in Washington, DC, from Chosen, Florida, which is 45 miles due west of Palm Beach and lies at the eastern edge of Lake Okeechobee. Gertie and her family built a home in Chosen (a small town between Belle Glade and Lake Okeechobee) and moved there in 1934/35. The family wanted to be closer to the farm and their beloved Lake Okeechobee.

Aftermath of the 1928 Hurricane

1. *Everglades in the vicinity of Belle Glade under water.*

2. *Utter destruction in West Palm Beach.*

3. *Loading bodies of those who perished in the Everglades into truck at Belle Glade. Ross Winne is standing on the left.*

2

Hurricane of 1949

August 26, 1949, 4:30 a.m.

A queer time to start a letter, but I may not have another moment's peace today. The latest hurricane raging up from the doldrums is just point 6° west, and warning flags are flying all up and down the Florida coast. If the storm continues its present course, it will hit Palm Beach dead center, and we will get a terrific jolt ourselves. Usually, though, when these storms strike the Gulf Stream they veer, so there's no point in predicting what will happen.

Cat Island in the Bahamas had winds up to 120 miles an hour, and it seems that the monster is spread out considerably. It's traveling very slowly, as all the dangerous ones do, but the Weather Bureau hasn't yet—or at least not that I have heard—given us the approximate diameter.

We've been out of bed half an hour now and have just listened to the Weather Bureau's 4 o'clock advisory on the storm. It's still black dark outside and the wind is blowing gustily. Waiting for a hurricane is the worst waiting I know. No matter how old you are, you never get used to it. I'd like to go back to bed, but I know I couldn't sleep, so I'll stop now and make a pot of coffee.

August 27, 1949, 11 a.m.

The storm passed over us last night. We are still here, and the house is here—in one piece but drenched in water. Outside the rain is still coming down in torrents, although not as much as last night when the storm was at its height. It rained so hard and the wind blew the rain up under the shingles so badly that the house was like a sieve.

About 11 o'clock yesterday morning, Dad thought it was time to board up, so he and Ross, Jr., began nailing boards across the windows. I started checking the canned goods, the bread, the eggs, and such, and after that, went outside for a look around. Dad and Ross had finished the shutters on the south side and were working on the east and north. They decided against boarding the west side—a bad mistake.

The wind was fresh, blowing from the north and, in the drainage ditches along the road the water was rising steadily as though something was driving it out of the ground. To escape the rising water, hundreds of tiny insects were crawling over the lawn looking for dry land. (Do you remember how the ants came crawling up from the water in 1928?)

A strange air of oppression hung over everything—the wind blowing and the cirrus clouds spread out in the sky and all of the trees a heavy, hard-shining green in that queer light. Thank heaven, I thought, that Dad and Ross, Jr., had just topped all the oaks close to the house.

Along the road as far as I could see everybody who had shutters was putting up shutters and storing movable items. Dad and Ross, Jr., had by then finished with our own shutters and were staking the little trees, tying them up so they wouldn't get too whipped about. I went inside and began putting things away in the back porch so that the wind and rain coming through those open screens wouldn't damage anything too much. I put a piece of canvas over my washing machine and tied it down. I laid the tools away in the cupboards, whatever I could get in.

Then Dot, Si, and Judith came (daughter, son-in-law, and 3-year-old grandchild). When Dot and Si got off work at noon, they went by their house and brought Judith's mattress and a few clothes and came here to stay. We all had a bite of lunch and washed up afterward. Then there wasn't much to do but wait and pray. Nobody said anything much. Every now and again we looked at the barometer, which was going down rapidly.

The wind began whooping in earnest about 4 o'clock and by 6 o'clock it was furious. The electricity went off at 7:12 p.m., according to the electric clock in the kitchen. We hauled out the oil lamps and a box of candles, so we had light inside, but outside it was so dark we couldn't see anything.

For about 3 hours then, we didn't know if the house would stay on the foundations. Judith had her arms tight around my neck and wouldn't let go. Even Dad said he was scared, which was very unusual. We all looked scared, so it was no use trying to deny it.

The first storm winds came in on us from the north-northeast. Then about 8:30, the wind hauled to the northeast and soon afterward to the west, then southwest, and then ... the roof began leaking like a sieve and the floor was soon awash. We started moving the furniture around, trying to keep it dry. We also had to shift the lamps constantly to keep the drops from falling on the hot chimneys, and even so, one of them got broken.

All the while, the roar of the storm was deafening. At every gust we heard the spiteful, crackling, whining wind coming nearer and nearer, clutching the house as if with mighty hands, shaking and rending until we could fairly hear the nails pulling from the wood. The house heaved and twisted, groaned and shuddered, and creaked; furniture on the back porch broke loose from its moorings and banged and rattled; branches from trees pelted the house, and small items from the machine shop next door flew and banged about the house. This, with the howl of the wind and the roar of the storm, was nerve-shattering and deafening.

About 11 o'clock when we were certain that worse was yet to come, the barometer started to rise and we began to breathe again. It had gone down to 28.41 inches. Around midnight the wind had died down a bit, and we lay down for a little rest. (Mercifully, the bedrooms were dry, but everything else was awash.) After 2 o'clock we all slept fitfully, but the wind howled until morning.

By 7:30 a.m. we were all out of bed. I hauled out the old faithful one-burner oil stove and had coffee ready at about 9 o'clock. I left the stove burning and kept the two oil lamps and half a dozen candles lit. Altogether, they helped dry out the house considerably, but it was still raining torrents outside.

Ross, Jr., and Si worked on the cars, trying to get them running. Finally they got them started, and the Seilers took their belongings and went home; Dad and Ross, Jr., went to Belle Glade to see if any papers came in. They have not come back yet. I imagine they drove out to Slim's (bridge-tender and lock-keeper at the government dike, gateway to three islands on Lake Okeechobee) for a look-see.

August 27, 1949, 4 p.m.

The rain has nearly stopped. Dad and Ross, Jr., did ride out to Slim's (also a boat and fishing camp). They say the country is a shambles. The wind drove the lake up to the 24½-foot elevation; the road at the island end of the bridge is badly washed. Slim's boats and all others that are kept out there broke loose, and what didn't sink drifted against the levee for no telling what distance. Part of Slim's dock shed went out, and he doesn't know how many of his kickers (outboard motors) are sunk or lost.

Dad said that looking out over the islands, the Braddock house is gone, no sign of it anywhere. The old Cromartie house is still standing. Our house on the farm washed off the foundation but is still there. Farther out, they could see nothing.

I'm afraid there are a lot of drowned cattle and horses out there. Harry Schug was here for a few minutes this morning. He said Fritz (Stein) had taken his cattle off the island but hadn't been able to get 10 horses off.

Things aren't too awful in Belle Glade. A few roofs are off, shingles and paper off some houses, and some houses are off the foundation, but apparently no one was injured.

West Palm Beach and Lake Worth are a shambles. Smiddy and Martha (son and daughter-in-law) drove in at 3 o'clock. They were in the center of the storm. The lull lasted an hour, and there was sustained wind of 140 miles an hour. At Morrison Homes where they live, the roofs blew off all the houses, and everything and everybody were out in the weather, drenched. They went in to Southridge (a public housing project at Southern Boulevard between Georgia and Lake Avenue), which is made of concrete and steel construction, right in the worst of the storm. Smiddy made three trips bringing in other families during the lull of the storm.

They said the radio reports about the Glades had them scared to death, so they came out to see for themselves. Starting out, they found the highway washed out east of Loxahatchee, so they went down the Rangeline Road to Fort Lauderdale (about 45 miles south of Palm Beach) and came out that way, a total of approximately 115 miles. Just this side of Lauderdale, a car ahead of them skidded and rolled over four times. A crowd of people soon collected, but no one wanted to do anything; everyone wanted to wait for the highway patrol. Smiddy said, "To hell with that! It may be hours before one can get here with telephones out and the patrol more than busy at a time like this." So he put the man in his car and took him to the hospital in Lauderdale, answered a thousand-and-one questions, then came on out.

Smiddy said that on the coast, particularly at West Palm Beach, store fronts are blown in and houses wrecked as badly as in 1928. They have called in the National Guard to help keep down the looting. At Boynton Beach, a school auditorium roof blew off and 60 people taking refuge there had to be evacuated at the height of the storm. Somewhere in West Palm Beach there were more than 200 people in a school auditorium when the roof blew off. We have had no word as yet on the number killed or injured.

Smiddy and Martha didn't stay long because they wanted to get back to West Palm Beach before night. They had left the children with a friend, Irene Williams.

August 28, 1949, 7 a.m.
Now it is Sunday morning, 7 o'clock. Dad and Ross, Jr., are still asleep. The weather looks quite promising; clear sky is showing

in patches, so we may have a bit of sun to help dry out the house, which is beginning to smell musty already.

When Ross (Dad) came home last night, he said he had gone with Harry looking for his boat. They found it drifted against the levee about a mile north of the bridge. There were broken oars, oil cans, boats, and all sorts of debris strewn along the dike. They saw the wreckage of the Braddock house, too, so I imagine the other island houses are scattered along the levee farther north. They said the lake (Okeechobee) had blown in to a 24.5 elevation (24½ feet above sea level.) Normally the lake stands at about 15 feet.

Anyway, they were fortunate in finding Harry's oars in his boat, so they got the boat down off the levee into the water and took it back down to Slim's, where Harry found his motor was still in the part of the shed that hadn't blown down. They managed to get the thing onto the boat and running, so they went over to Rabbit Island to look over Harry's celery seed beds. He thinks he can save most of them.

When they came back, they stopped at Fritz's. He had gone to Kreamer Island in a boat yesterday afternoon. He said that the twin bridges over the pass between Torry and Kreamer Islands had washed away; the Ives house and other buildings are gone, and all of his dikes are gone—$400,000 worth of dikes. He had managed to get his cattle off the island before the storm but had eight horses that he couldn't get, so he lost those.

Dad went on over to Harry's to eat supper with him. When he came home he said that Helen Schug had been down to the Kruses' yesterday afternoon, and the lovely big windows in the front of Frank's house had blown out; they took doors off the closets and nailed them over the openings to keep the wind out. I guess this is another time when Frank wishes he didn't have so much house and had a bit of that $80,000 in his jeans instead. The Kruse brothers had 300 acres of corn that they were to have started gathering in a week or so. Corn has been a good price, so that is quite a loss.

It is now 11 o'clock. I have a bit of washing on the line and several things out to dry. As soon as we get electricity, I'll really put out a big one. My floors are still wet under the linoleum, but I think they will dry before long because we have a nice breeze and the sun is shining most of the time. It's really a good drying day.

Mail came in, and Ross brought some for the Seilers, so the card I sent you yesterday must have got off. You should get it tomorrow, I hope. I must write others. If I could get word to you any quicker I would, but the storm cut a wide swath clear across the state, so communication from South Florida is pretty well cut off.

September 4, 1949

This week Army engineers from Jacksonville and Washington examined the levee, clucking in surprise. They agree that if the wind had lasted another hour, the levee would have gone out, and a wall of water would have flooded the Everglades, as in 1928.

Many people are comparing last week's storm with what happened then (1928), and they say this one did more damage. Perhaps they are right, from the dollar and cents standpoint, because there are dollars invested here today that were merely pennies then. But how can anyone begin to compare the dollar damage to the terrible loss of life that we had in that other storm when entire families were wiped out and there were few who did not lose some loved one?

Conclusion

In many respects, my family has been fortunate. During the hurricane of September 18, 1928, we all managed to stay together. That storm too came to the Everglades in the night time. In those days the warning system was not so highly developed as it is today. Radios were rather new, and not many homes had them. We relied mostly on our own knowledge of wind and weather.

I must say that the hurricane of 1949 cannot even begin to compare in any way with that other tragedy of 1928. Such comparisons always come easily from those who did not live through both, as we did. Even today, these many years after, the tears of 1928 are never far away; and so long as we live and have memory, we will remember the pain, and the loss, and the sorrow.

Ross and Gertrude, 40th wedding anniversary

Epilogue

Gertrude and Ross Winne remained in the Glades for the remainder of their lives. The devastating loss of life in the 1928 hurricane prompted the construction of an earthen dam around the lake. The Flood Control District was also formed and the US Army Corps of Engineers constructed a series of locks and floodgates around the lake to prevent a recurrence of the devastation and tragedy of 1928.

Hurricane Andrew struck the southern tip of Florida from south of Miami to Homestead and across the state in August 1992. The hurricane continued to plow through the Gulf of Mexico with undiminished fury and slammed into the Louisiana coast. Although property damage was the highest in recorded history at that time, loss of life was less than 30 souls. The modern miracles of hurricane reconnaissance, satellite surveillance, expert weather forecasters, and radio and television news bulletins prevented the serious loss of life suffered in 1928.

About the Author

Gertrude Marie Petersen was born February 7, 1892, in Elliston, Benton Township, Ottawa County, Ohio. She was one of 11 children. Her mother and family emigrated from Germany. On June 10, 1910, she married Ross Wesley Winne, who was born January 22, 1882, in the former town of Nina, Carroll Township, Ottawa County, Ohio. Before leaving Ohio, Ross was a commercial fisherman and hunter (mainly ducks) on Lake Erie. He died on October 30, 1960, at the age of 78 years. Gertrude died June 27, 1972, in West Palm Beach, Florida, at the age of 80 years.

About the Editor

Patricia Winne Adams was born in Chosen, Florida (now commonly known as Belle Glade) in the home of Ross and Gertrude Winne. Her parents, Herman and Martha were then living in the small house on Torry Island that was built after the 1928 hurricane (shown on the cover of this book). Patricia graduated from Palm Beach High School in West Palm Beach, Florida and attained an Associate Degree in Personnel Management from Vernon Regional Junior College, Wichita Falls, Texas in 1992. She was a civil service employee with the US Air Force for 28 years followed by 2½ years with the US Navy prior to her retirement in 1997. She and her husband Jack now live on the western shore of Lake Okeechobee about 40 minutes from her place of birth.